A PARENT'S SURVIVAL GUIDE TO MATHS HOMEWORK

Make sense of your kid's maths

ANDREW BRODIE

Published 2010 by A&C Black Publishers Limited
36 Soho Square, London W1D 3QY
www.acblack.com

ISBN 978-1-4081-248-57

A CIP record for this publication is available from the British Library.

Printed in Great Britain by Martins the Printers, Berwick-upon-Tweed

This book is produced using paper that is made from wood grown in managed, sustainable forests. It is natural, renewable and recyclable. The logging and manufacturing processes conform to the environmental regulations of the country of origin.

To see our full range of titles visit www.acblack.com

Contents

Why do you need this book? ... 4

What happens in school? ... 5

What maths will my child be learning? ... 5

What equipment do I need to help? ... 6

Maths in the Foundation Stage ... 8

Maths in Year 1 ... 14

Maths in Year 2 ... 22

Maths in Year 3 ... 34

Maths in Year 4 ... 45

Maths in Year 5 ... 60

Maths in Year 6 ... 77

Useful books ... 96

? Why do you need this book?

Whether you are a maths whizz or find it all a little daunting, this is the book for you. It will tell you all you need to know about the maths that is being taught to your child in school. You will soon learn, for example, when your child will start to learn times-tables and how you can support this at home. It will also help to reveal the mysteries of how maths is taught today. You may find that things have changed a little since you were a child!

Is this a familiar scene in your home? Which answer are you most likely to give?

Helping your child with maths is one of the most useful things you can do for them. It will help them with their learning in many other subjects in school and will be a great step-up into life beyond school.

What happens in school?

In England, schools are separated into three phases: Foundation Stage, Key Stage 1 and Key Stage 2. You can see at a glance how your child will fit into each phase in the chart opposite:

Foundation Stage	Reception	Up to age 5
Key Stage 1	Year 1	Age 5-6
	Year 2	Age 6-7
Key Stage 2	Year 3	Age 7-8
	Year 4	Age 8-9
	Year 5	Age 9-10
	Year 6	Age 10-11

What maths will my child be learning?

Throughout their primary years, your child will be learning all kinds of maths. Here's a handy guide to what it all means:

Jargon-busting guide

Using and applying mathematics	How maths can be used in everyday life, from dealing with money to working out how long a TV programme lasts.
Counting and understanding number	From how to count chocolate buttons to working out what fraction of a pizza each person should have.
Knowing and using number facts	Knowing off by heart facts such as 3 + 2 = 5 and, as your child gets older, learning all the multiplication tables.
Calculating	How to add up, take away, multiply and divide. Older children will learn how to find fractions and percentages, such as 45% of £60.
Understanding shape	Learning the names of shapes and later, how to measure angles.
Measuring	How to measure lengths, weights and so on and also how to tell the time.
Handling data	Learning how to sort objects by colour or size and later, how to draw or interpret graphs and pie charts.

Special note!
The most important aspect is **Using and applying mathematics** simply because there is no point in children knowing lots of number facts unless they are able to use them in real-life situations.

? What equipment do I need to help?

You can help your child with maths using everyday things that you can find in your home. There is no need to buy expensive equipment! The following will be really handy:

- Chocolate buttons – for all sorts of counting activities, a great way to motivate your child!

- Measuring jugs – from your kitchen cupboard or your child might like to make one, using a clean plastic milk carton.

- Small toys such as toy cars and lorries for sorting and counting.

- Cups, mugs and plates for counting and sharing.

- Socks! Ideal for beginning to understand doubling and the 2 times-table.

- Books or CD cases for simple adding or taking away.

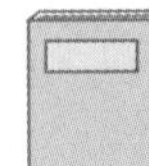

- Drinking straws, for making shapes such as triangles.

- Scissors, but not too sharp!

- Number lines that you can make yourself (see opposite).
- Blank cards for writing numbers on.
- A clock with clear numbers.

As your child gets older:

- Rulers and measuring tapes.
- Protractor.
- Coins.

Number lines can be very helpful for all ages of children when they are learning maths as they can see clearly what's happening as they add or subtract. At the early stages, simply draw a line then mark 10 or 20 blobs on it at regular intervals numbered 1 to 10 or 1 to 20.

When your child is a bit older you can create a line from 0 to 40 or from 0 to 100. Some schools will use 'empty number lines' as the children get older - with these the children can mark on the numbers they need.

Maths in the Foundation Stage

If your child is in their Reception year they will be expected to achieve targets for each aspect of mathematics. These are shown below, with some quick and easy ways to help your child to learn through play at home.

? What are the targets?

Using and applying mathematics

- ★ Match sets of objects to numbers.
- ★ Sort objects.
- ★ Recognise and talk about simple patterns.

Make a pattern of toy cars together, try two cars, one lorry, two cars, one lorry. What other patterns can your child think of?

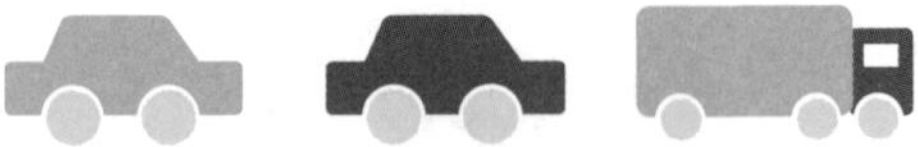

- ★ Use mathematical ideas and methods to solve practical problems.

When you write the number four do it as an open '4' as this is the way your child will learn the number at school.

Counting and understanding numbers

- ★ Say the number names in order up to at least 10.
- ★ Recognise numbers from 1 to 9.

1 2 3 4 5 6 7 8 9

- ★ Count up to 10 objects.
- ★ Count aloud in ones, twos, fives or tens.
- ★ Talk about 'more' or 'less' to compare two numbers.

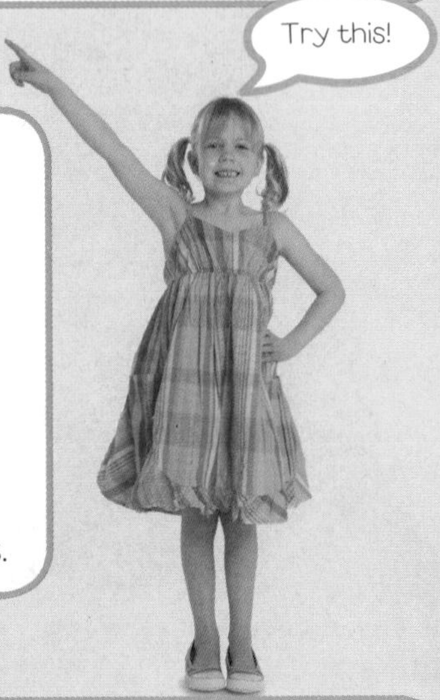

Knowing and using number facts

- ★ Find one more or one less than a number.
- ★ Select two groups of objects to make a given total of objects.

Ask your child to help you lay the table. Put one plate out. Ask, 'How many more do we need so everyone has one plate?'

Calculating

★ Begin to understand addition as combining two groups of objects.

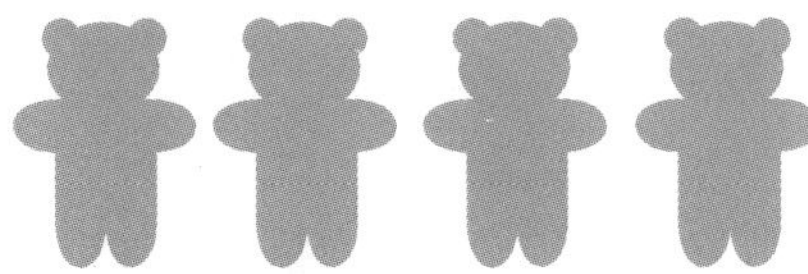

Four bears and two more bears make six bears altogether.

★ Begin to understand subtraction as 'taking away'.

★ Count repeated groups of the same size.

★ Share objects into equal groups.

Share a small bunch of grapes with your child. Count how many you have each. Can you both have the same number or is there one left over?

Understanding shape

★ Describe the shape and size of solids and flat shapes.

★ Describe position, using words such as over, under, above, below, middle, edge, corner and so on.

Talk about any tables you have in your house. 'What shape is the coffee table? How many sides has the top got? How many corners has the top got?'

Measuring

★ When measuring, compare quantities using language such as 'greater' or 'smaller' and 'heavier' or 'lighter'.

★ Talk about time, using everyday language such as the days of the week.

Ask your child questions, such as: 'What day is it today? What do we do every Saturday? What do we do every Sunday? What happens every Monday?'

Handling data

★ Sort familiar objects to identify their similarities and differences.

★ Count how many objects there are with a particular property and use pictures or numbers to present the results.

? How else can I help at home?

It's important to make maths as much fun as possible and to use lots of repetition. Talk to your child's class teacher to ensure that you both know what your child is practising.

Learning numbers up to 9

Take every opportunity to say or sing counting rhymes together. Try:

One, two, three, four, five,
Once I caught a fish alive.
Six, seven, eight, nine, ten,
Then I let it go again.

One, two, buckle my shoe.
Three, four, knock at the door.
Five, six, pick up sticks.
Seven, eight, shut the gate.
Nine, ten, a big fat hen.

One potato, two potato,
Three potato, four.
Five potato, six potato,
Seven potato, more.

One, two, three, four,
I will knock on your front door.
Five, six, seven, eight,
I hope you're in as we are late.

Games around the house

Talk about the numbers one to nine as much as you can. Try these games:

- point at the numbers as you sing number rhymes together
- count cups as you put them out for drinks
- count the chocolate buttons in a packet
- count the stairs on the way up and on the way down
- count the toys as you put them away
- ask your child to put the numbers 1 to 9 in order using plastic numbers or fridge magnets.

Activity ideas Number line

Make a colourful number line by writing the numbers 1 to 9 on separate sheets of paper. Ask your child to decorate these using pens, paints and even glitter! Attach the numbers with clothes pegs to a piece of string (make sure they are in the correct order!). Display your number line on a wall or across a room from one piece of furniture to another. Talk about the numbers by asking your child to:

- count up to six
- count back from nine
- say which number is one more than seven
- say which number is one less than five
- sing 'counting back' songs such as 'Ten in the Bed' and 'Five Little Ducks'.

Going beyond number 9

Once your child is confident with the numbers one to nine, extend their skills by looking at ten and beyond:

Change your number line to one that shows numbers from 1 to 20. Try the following ideas:

- count up to 16
- count back from 17
- say which number is one less than 14
- say which number is one more than 11

Activity ideas Questions and answers

What you need:

five apples, seven books, packet of chocolate buttons, three bowls.

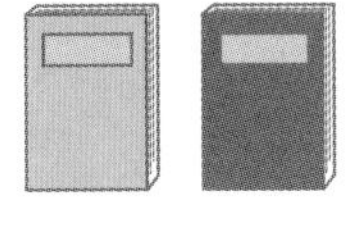

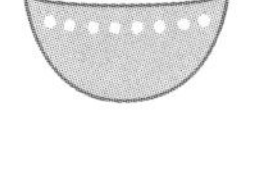

What to do:

Give your child some questions, using real objects so that they can move them around easily to find the answers. Try these then make up some of your own:

Addition

- 'Here are three apples. If we get two more apples, how many will we have altogether?' (Make sure you have a total of five apples ready.)
- 'There are four books in this pile and three books in that pile. What is the total number of books?'

Subtraction:

- 'If we have five apples and we eat one of them, how many apples will there be?'
- 'There are eight chocolate buttons in the bowl. If we eat five of them, how many will there be in the bowl then?'

Multiplication:

- 'Here are three bowls. There are two chocolate buttons in each bowl. How many chocolate buttons are there altogether?'

Division:

- 'Here are ten chocolate buttons. Let's share them so that both of us have the same number. How many buttons have we each got?'

Now challenge your child to ask you some questions – they will love this!

Looking at shapes

Children in Reception will learn about the following 2-D (two-dimensional) shapes:

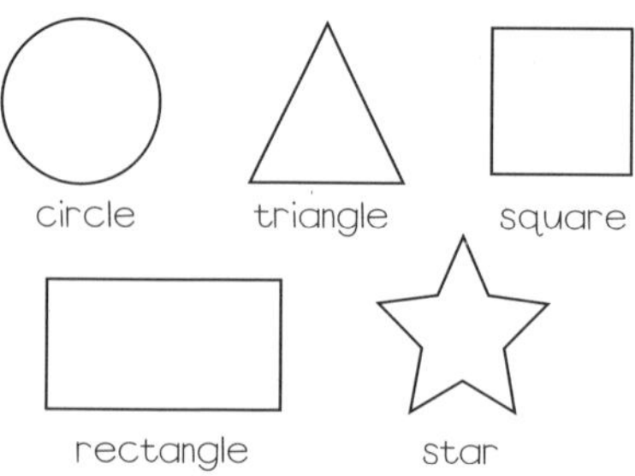

They will learn about these 3-D (three-dimensional) shapes:

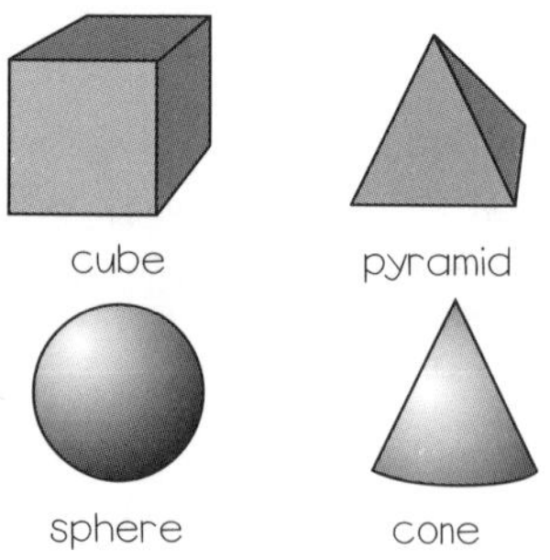

Games around the home

Talk about shapes as much as you can. Try these games:

- Look at shapes around your home. Ask, 'What shape are these tiles on the floor?', 'What shape is the flat end of this tin?', 'What shape is the face of each brick we can see in this wall?'
- Make shapes together using drinking straws – what shape do three drinking straws make?

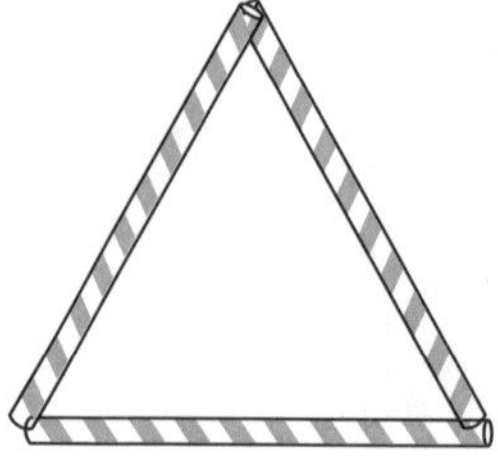

– if you cut one of the straws in half, what shape can you make now?

– what shape do four drinking straws make?

- Collect different shapes from around your home, such as boxes, tins and cereal packets. Talk about the different shapes then ask your child to make something out of them: what about a castle, a robot, a car or their own idea?

Position

In the Reception class your child will be encouraged to learn about position, direction and movement.

Useful words

Help at home by finding opportunities to use vocabulary such as:

- over, under
- above, below, between
- top, bottom, side
- in front, behind
- front, back
- before, after
- middle, edge, corner
- left, right
- up, down

How about going on your own 'Bear Hunt' around the house? Read *We're Going on a Bear Hunt* by Michael Rosen (Walker Books) then move around the house together using as many of the 'position' words above as you can.

Measuring

Help your child to make comparisons between everyday objects. Prompt them whenever you spot an opportunity:

Who has the most dinner?

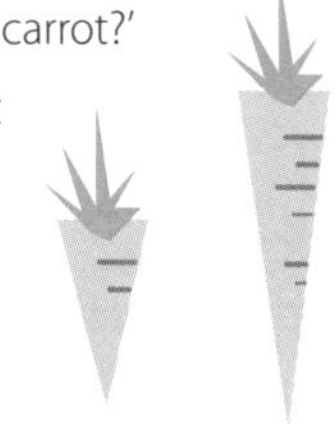

- 'Which is the longest carrot?'
- 'Which is the shortest carrot?'
- 'Who is the tallest?'
- 'Who is the shortest?'
- 'Which is the tallest teddy?'
- 'Which is the shortest teddy?'

- 'Which glass is full?'
- 'Which glass is half full?'
- 'Which glass is empty?'

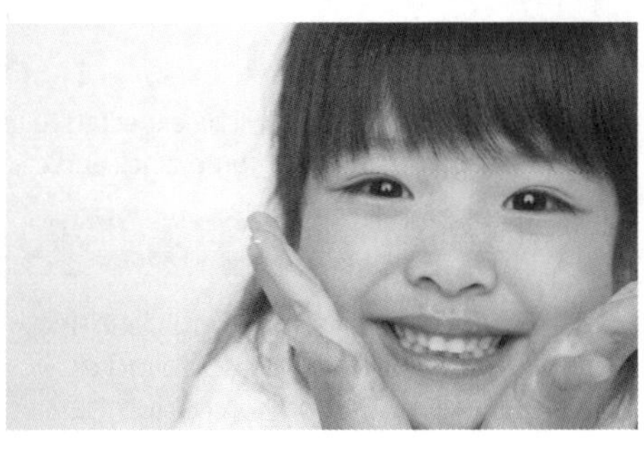

Time

The whole concept of 'time' is very difficult for young children to grasp. Talk about time in very general terms. Ask questions such as:

- 'What day is it today?' 'What did we do today?'
- 'What day was it yesterday?' 'What did we do yesterday?'
- 'What day will it be tomorrow?' 'What would you like to do tomorrow?'

Useful words

Whenever you can, use other 'time' vocabulary such as:

- morning
- afternoon
- evening
- night
- day
- week
- birthday
- o'clock
- clock
- hands

... and if your Reception age child finds everything easy, have a look at what children are taught in Year 1.

Maths in Year 1

If your child is in Year 1 they will be expected to achieve targets for each aspect of mathematics. These are shown below, along with some quick and easy ways to help your child with maths at home.

Using and applying mathematics

- ★ Solve problems involving counting, adding, subtracting, doubling or halving in the context of numbers, money or measures.
- ★ Describe a puzzle or problem using numbers, practical materials and diagrams then use these to solve the problem.
- ★ Choose suitable equipment to help answer a question.
- ★ Display results using tables or pictures.

Draw three triangles, a square, a rectangle and a star all on separate pieces of paper. Ask your child to sort them into 'triangles' and 'not triangles'.

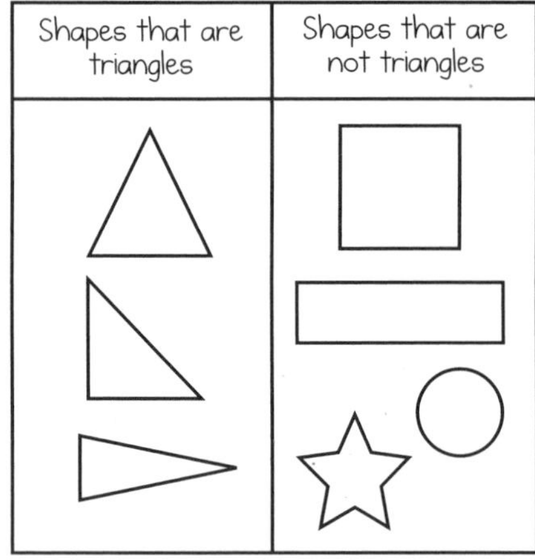

- ★ Describe simple patterns and relationships involving numbers or shapes.

Counting and understanding numbers

- ★ Count at least 20 objects without making errors.
- ★ Estimate a number of objects then check by counting.
- ★ Compare numbers and put them in order, using vocabulary such as more, bigger, greater, fewer, smaller, less and so on.

Write out the numbers 0 to 20 on separate small cards. Pick any two cards and ask your child which shows the bigger number.

- ★ Use the equals sign (=).
- ★ Read and write numbers from 0 to 20, then beyond. Position the numbers on a number track or a number line.
- ★ Say the number that is 1 more or 1 less than any given number.

Write out the numbers 0 to 20 on separate small cards. Show your child any card and ask what number is one more than the number on the card.

- ★ Say the number that is 10 more or 10 less than any multiple of 10.
- ★ Talk about halves and quarters.

Knowing and using number facts

★ Find all pairs of numbers with a total of 10, then remember these number pairs.

★ Find and remember addition facts for totals to at least 5.

Your child needs to practise and learn number facts such as:
1 + 4 = 5   2 + 3 = 5
3 + 2 = 5   4 + 1 = 5

★ Work out the subtraction facts that correspond to the addition facts.

★ Count on in ones, twos, fives and tens. Count back in ones, twos, fives and tens.

★ Find the multiples of 2, 5 and 10 to the tenth multiple (that is, up to ten times).

★ Remember the doubles of all numbers to at least 10.

Calculating

★ Relate addition to 'counting on'. Recognise that addition can be done in any order.

★ Understand subtraction as 'taking away' and as 'finding a difference' by counting up.

★ Use practical and informal written methods to help when adding or subtracting.

★ Use appropriate vocabulary for addition and subtraction. Use symbols to write addition and subtraction number sentences.

Write + on one card and = on another. Challenge your child to use these with your number cards to make some addition sentences.

This number sentence uses the addition symbol and the equals symbol.

★ Solve practical problems that involve combining groups of 2, 5 or 10. (This is the early stage of understanding multiplication.)

★ Solve practical problems that involve sharing into equal groups. (This is the early stage of understanding division.)

Understanding shape

- ★ Identify common 2-D (two-dimensional) shapes and describe their features.

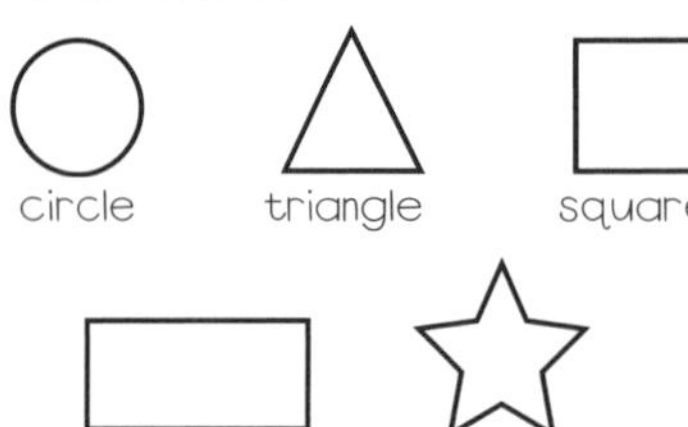

- ★ Identify common 3-D (three-dimensional) solids and describe their features.
- ★ Use shapes to make patterns, pictures and models.
- ★ Identify objects that turn about a point.
- ★ Recognise and make whole turns, half turns and quarter turns.
- ★ Describe the position of objects.
- ★ Describe direction and distance when moving objects such as pieces on a game board.

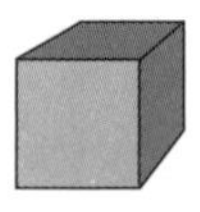
Cube

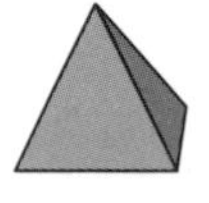
pyramid

sphere

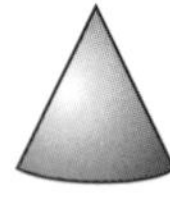
cone

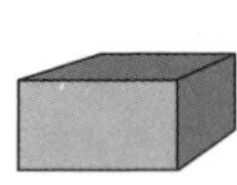
cuboid

cylinder

Measuring

- ★ Estimate weights of objects by comparing them.
- ★ Estimate lengths of objects by comparing them.
- ★ Weigh objects using suitable non-standard or standard units.

Standard units of measurement are those that always remain the same such as grams, kilometres and centimetres. Non-standard units could be anything else that you use to measure, such as pebbles or the length of your stride!

- ★ Measure the lengths of objects using suitable non-standard or standard units.
- ★ Talk about time. Say the days of the week and the months of the year in order.
- ★ Read the time on an analogue clock (not digital) for o'clock and half-past times.

★ Answer a question by recording information in lists and tables.

★ Show outcomes using practical resources, pictures, block graphs or pictograms.

Here are two ways of showing how many people prefer apples and how many prefer bananas. Your child can see that there were six people altogether and that four preferred apples and two preferred bananas.

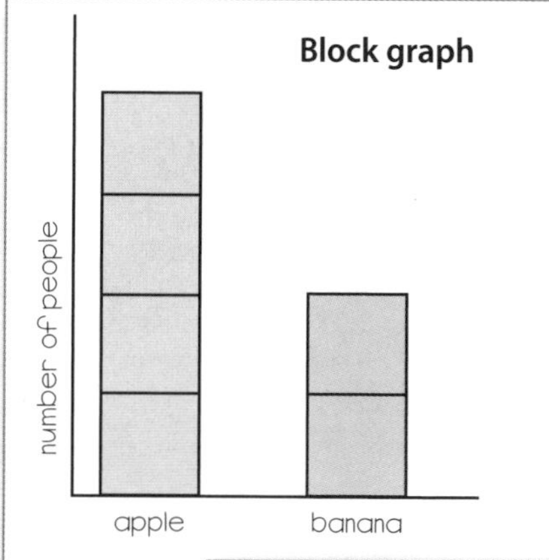

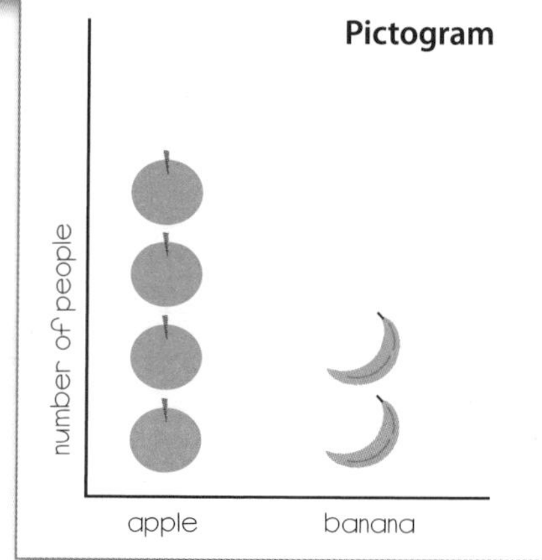

★ Use diagrams to sort objects into groups.

How else can I help at home?

It's important to make maths as much fun as possible and to use lots of repetition. Talk to your child's class teacher to ensure that you know what your child should be practising.

Using and applying mathematics

Food for thought

To encourage your child in 'using and applying mathematics' talk about maths as much as you can in everyday life. For example, when sharing out food discuss and compare quantities, ask:

'Who has the biggest piece of pizza?'

'Watch me cut the pizza in half. Now I'm going to cut it in quarters.'

Understanding numbers

Games around the home

Keep up the practice of counting whenever possible. Count:

- the number of plates on the table
- the number of books on a shelf
- the number of CDs in the rack
- the number of sweets in a packet.

Also encourage the idea of estimating before counting.

Activity ideas Number line

Make a colourful number line showing the numbers from 0-40. You could tape pieces of paper together or use the back of an old piece of wallpaper (draw a long line and write the numbers underneath at regular intervals). Get your child to decorate the number line as they wish. Put it up at child height and talk about the numbers by asking your child to:

- identify the number you point to
- say which number is one more than 17
- say which number is one less than 25
- say which number is ten more than 20
- say which number is ten less than 40
- count in twos from 2 to 20, then beyond
- count in fives from 5 to 40
- count in tens from 10 to 40.

If you feel that your child is ready, you could count together in tens starting at 10 then going all the way to 100.

Draw 'number spikes' (as below) and find pairs of numbers that total the number in the centre. Here is a number spike for 5 and a number spike for 7:

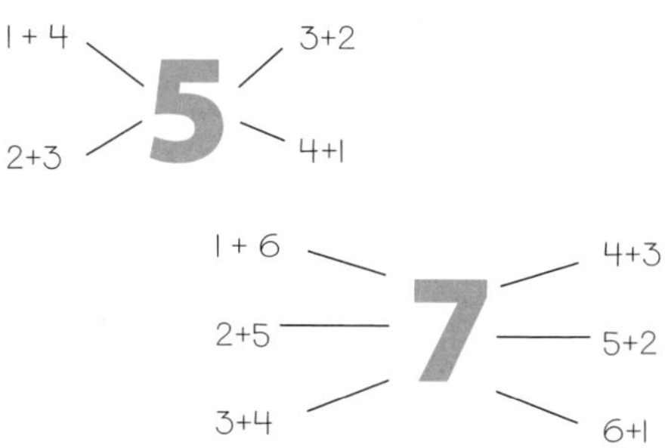

Encourage your child to start from the larger number when counting on. For example, if they have to answer the question 3 + 7, encourage them to start with the 7 then make three jumps.

It's still a good idea to continue using practical equipment to practise adding. This could include pencils, sweets, fruit, toys, erasers, leaves, flowers and so on.

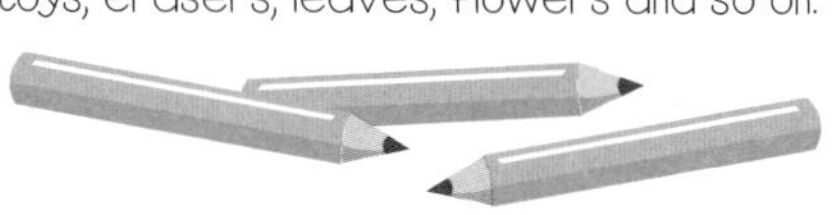

Addition

Use your number line to help your child to count on. Ask questions such as 6 + 5, then encourage your child to find the number 6 on the number line and to make five 'jumps' from number to number to find the answer – they should, of course, find the answer 11.

Practice makes perfect so keep asking questions such as:

7 + 5	8 + 2	4 + 3
9 + 6	8 + 5	7 + 6

Useful words

Use a variety of 'maths' vocabulary, all related to addition, such as:

- 'six **add** four'
- 'what number is four **more than** six?'
- 'six **plus** four'
- 'what is the **total** of six and four?'
- '**how much** is six and four **altogether**?'
- 'what is the **sum** of six and four?'

Activity ideas Double trouble

What you need: six spoons from your cutlery drawer.

What to do

Talk about doubles. First of all, check that your child understands what a double is. Put two spoons on the table. Ask your child how many spoons there would be if there were double the number they can see. Now put two more spoons on the table and talk about how many there are now. Remind your child that there were two spoons but you've doubled the number of spoons so there are now four. Play again but start with three spoons on the table.

When you are sure that your child understands the concept, start practising doubles by asking questions such as:

- 'What's double three?'
- 'What's double one?'
- 'What's double four?'
- 'What's double six?'

Subtraction

Carry on using practical equipment such as toys or food and appropriate vocabulary to practise subtracting:

- 'what is eight **take away** six?'
- 'what is eight **subtract** six?'
- '**take** six **from** eight'
- 'what is eight **minus** six?'

Finding the difference

When you feel that your child is confident with the concept of subtraction, move on to 'finding the difference'. Here the number line is very useful again.

Ask, 'What is the difference between nine and four?'

Show your child how to start at the number 4, then to count the number of 'jumps' to reach 9.

Multiplication

It's a very good idea to continue using practical equipment:

- 'I've got five pairs of socks. How many socks are there altogether?'
- 'Here are three bowls. There are five raisins in each bowl. How many raisins are there altogether?'

Division

- 'Here are twelve grapes. If we share them between three people how many would each person have?'
- 'If we share them between two people how many would each person have?'
- 'If we share them between four people how many would each person have?'

Looking at shapes

Talk about shapes asking questions such as:

'What shape is the front of this box?'

'What type of solid shape is the box?' (Has your child learnt the name cuboid yet?)

'What shape is the end of this tin?'

'What type of solid shape is the tin?' (Has your child learnt the name cylinder yet?)

Useful words

Help at home by finding opportunities to use vocabulary such as:

- shape
- flat
- curved
- straight
- solid
- corner
- face
- side
- edge
- end
- point

Your child will be learning about position, direction and movement. When you can, use words such as:

- over, under, underneath
- above, below, between
- top, bottom, side
- in front, behind
- front, back
- before, after
- middle, edge, corner
- left, right
- up, down
- turn, whole turn, half turn

Measuring

Encourage your child to make comparisons of everyday objects. Ask:

'Which do you think is heavier, the potato or the carrot?'

Encourage your child to put pencils in order of length, from shortest to longest.

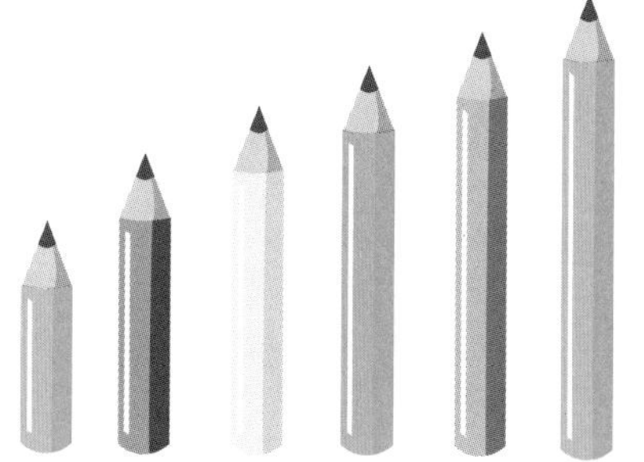

Talk about time

Help your child to grasp the concept of time by talking about the days of the week, for example:

- 'What day is it today? What did we do today?'
- 'What day was it yesterday? What did we do yesterday?'
- 'What day will it be tomorrow? 'What would you like to do tomorrow?'
- 'Tell me the days of the week in order.'

Draw their attention to the weather.

'What season is it now?'

'What is the weather like at this time of year?'

'Is it warm or cold?'

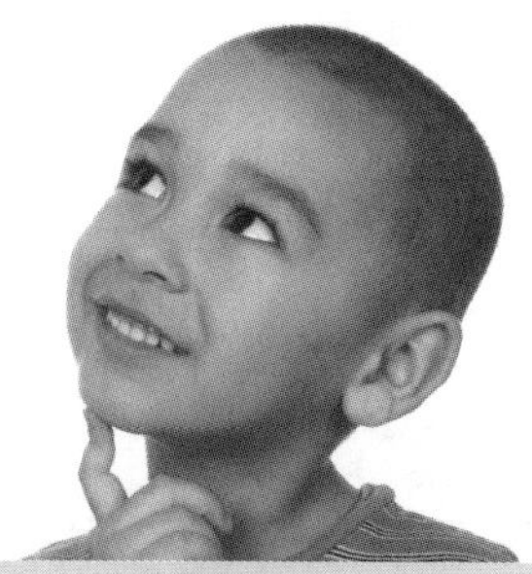

Useful words

Use other time vocabulary such as:

- morning
- afternoon
- evening
- night
- day
- week
- weekend
- birthday
- o'clock
- clock
- midnight
- half past
- hands

... and if your Year 1 child finds everything easy, have a look at what children are taught in Year 2.

Maths in Year 2

If your child is in Year 2 they will be expected to achieve targets for each aspect of mathematics. These are shown below, with some quick and easy ways of helping your child with maths at home.

Using and applying mathematics

★ Solve problems involving addition, subtraction, multiplication or division in the context of numbers, measures or money.

Label some fruit with prices: apple 40p, banana 60p, orange 30p. Talk about how much change you would have from £1 if you bought an apple, orange or banana. Then ask, 'What would two pieces of fruit cost? What change would there be? Have we enough money to buy all three pieces of fruit?'

★ Identify and write down the information or calculation needed to solve a puzzle or problem. Carry out the calculations and check the answer.

★ Choose suitable equipment to help to answer a question.

★ Select, organize and present information in lists, tables and simple diagrams.

★ Describe patterns and relationships involving numbers or shapes.

★ Make predictions and test these with examples.

★ Present solutions to puzzles and problems in an organized way.

★ Use mathematical language and number sentences.

Counting and understanding numbers

★ Read and write two-digit and three-digit numbers in figures and words.

★ Describe and extend number sequences.

A number sequence is a set of numbers following a particular pattern. Can your child spot the pattern in this sequence: 5, 10, 15, 20, 25...? What is the next number in this sequence?

★ Recognise odd and even numbers.

★ Count up to 100 objects by grouping them and counting in tens, fives or twos.

★ Explain what each digit in a two-digit number represents.

★ Put two-digit numbers in order. Find their position on a number line.

★ Use the greater than (>) and less than (<) signs.

★ Estimate a number of objects.

★ Round two-digit numbers to the nearest 10.

★ Find half, quarter and three quarters of shapes and sets of objects.

Knowing and using number facts

- ★ Find all addition and subtraction facts for each number to at least 10. Remember these facts.
- ★ Find and remember all pairs of numbers with totals to 20.
- ★ Find and remember all pairs of multiples of 10 with totals up to 100.
- ★ Find and remember the doubles of all numbers to 20. Understand that halving is the opposite or 'inverse' of doubling.
- ★ Learn the 2 times, the 5 times and the 10 times-tables.

1 x 2 = 2	1 x 5 = 5	1 x 10 = 10
2 x 2 = 4	2 x 5 = 10	2 x 10 = 20
3 x 2 = 6	3 x 5 = 15	3 x 10 = 30
4 x 2 = 8	4 x 5 = 20	4 x 10 = 40
5 x 2 = 10	5 x 5 = 25	5 x 10 = 50
6 x 2 = 12	6 x 5 = 30	6 x 10 = 60
7 x 2 = 14	7 x 5 = 35	7 x 10 = 70
8 x 2 = 16	8 x 5 = 40	8 x 10 = 80
9 x 2 = 18	9 x 5 = 45	9 x 10 = 90
10 x 2 = 20	10 x 5 = 50	10 x 10 = 100

- ★ Find the division facts that match these times-tables.
- ★ Recognise multiples of 2, 5 and 10.

Calculating

- ★ Add or subtract mentally a one-digit number or a multiple of 10 to or from any two-digit number.
- ★ Use practical and informal written methods to add and subtract two-digit numbers.
- ★ Understand that subtraction is the opposite, or 'inverse' of addition.
- ★ Find related addition and subtraction sentences.
- ★ Represent repeated addition as multiplication.
- ★ Represent arrays as multiplication.

An array is a set of objects formed into rows and columns. Each column has the same number of objects as the other columns and each row does likewise.

An array could look like this:

This array can show 4 sets of 3 or 3 sets of 4

☐	☐	☐	☐
☐	☐	☐	☐
☐	☐	☐	☐

- ★ Represent sharing or repeated subtraction as division.
- ★ Use practical and informal written methods to help with multiplication and division.
- ★ Use the symbols +, -, x, ÷ and = to make number sentences.
- ★ Calculate the value of an unknown in a number sentence. **6 + ☐ = 11**

Understanding shape

★ Identify common 2-D (two-dimensional) shapes from pictures of them in different positions (as shown below).

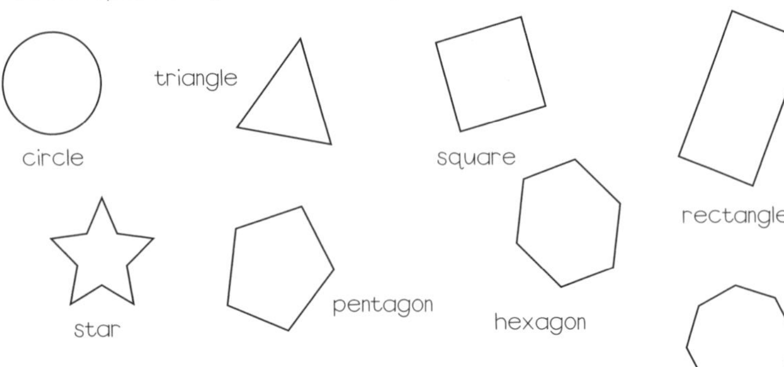

Draw some shapes on blank cards. Use them as flashcards – ask your child to tell you the name of the shape, the number of sides it has and the number of corners it has.

★ Identify common 3-D (three-dimensional) solids from pictures of them in different positions.

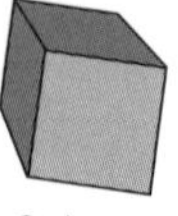

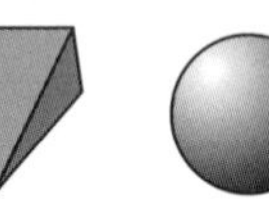

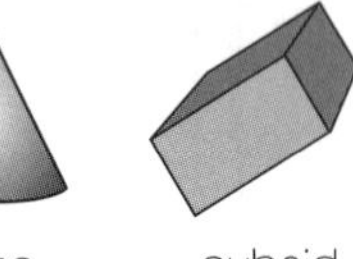

★ Sort, make and describe shapes, referring to their properties.

★ Identify reflective symmetry and draw lines of symmetry in shapes.

★ Follow and give instructions involving position, direction and movement.

★ Make whole, half and quarter turns, both clockwise and anti-clockwise.

★ Know that a right angle represents a quarter turn.

Measuring

- Estimate weights of objects by comparing them.
- Estimate lengths of objects by comparing them.
- Estimate capacities.
- Use standard units (metre, centimetre, kilogram, litre) with suitable measuring instruments.
- Read the numbered divisions on a scale and interpret the divisions between them.

When cooking, use scales that your child can read with you for measuring out quantities.

- Use a ruler to draw and measure lines to the nearest centimetre.
- Know the relationships between seconds, minutes, hours and days.
- Read the time on an analogue (not digital) clock for o'clock, half-past, quarter to and quarter past times.

Handling data

- Answer a question by recording information in lists and tables.
- Present outcomes using block graphs or pictograms.

Look at page 17 to see examples of a block graph and a pictogram .

- Use ICT to organize and present data.

If you have a spreadsheet program such as Excel on your home computer, experiment with your child to see how it can create simple graphs and charts.

- Use lists, tables and diagrams to sort objects into groups.

How else can I help at home?

It's important to make maths as much fun as possible and to use lots of repetition. Talk to your child's class teacher to ensure that you know what your child should be practising.

Using and applying mathematics

Everyday maths

Take every opportunity to talk about maths in everyday life:

- 'This packet of biscuits costs 46 pence. What change will I have if I pay for it with a 50 pence coin?'
- 'There are twelve cakes in this cake tin. If we eat three cakes, how many cakes will be left?'
- 'We need some ribbon to go around the birthday cake. Let's measure round the cake with a tape measure to see how much ribbon we need.'

Understanding numbers

Keep up the practice of estimating and counting whenever possible.

Use food such as cakes and pizzas to look at fractions with your child. Talk to them about half, quarter and three quarters.

Odd and even numbers

Ask questions such as:

- 'Can you find all the odd numbers less than 20?'
- 'Show me the even numbers between 39 and 61?'

Help your child to notice that odd numbers always have 1 or 3 or 5 or 7 or 9 as the units digit (note: some schools will call this the ones digit) and that even numbers always have 2 or 4 or 6 or 8 or 0 as the units digit.

Activity ideas Hundred square

Make a colourful hundred square with your child by drawing a ten by ten grid and writing the numbers 1 to 100 in each square. Stick it up on a wall or have it on the table where you can both see it. It will give you lots of opportunities for talking about maths.

1	2	3	4	5	6	7	8	9	10
11	12	13	14	15	16	17	18	19	20
21	22	23	24	25	26	27	28	29	30
31	32	33	34	35	36	37	38	39	40
41	42	43	44	45	46	47	48	49	50
51	52	53	54	55	56	57	58	59	60
61	62	63	64	65	66	67	68	69	70
71	72	73	74	75	76	77	78	79	80
81	82	83	84	85	86	87	88	89	90
91	92	93	94	95	96	97	98	99	100

Number sequences

Ask your child,

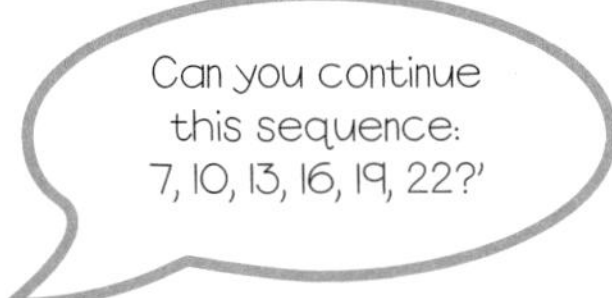

Does your child notice that the sequence is going up in threes? Use the hundred square to show this, taking particular care as you reach the end of each row.

Rounding numbers

Ask your child,

'Can you round to the nearest ten?'

Use lots of different numbers. The hundred square (or a number line to 100, see page 7 for how to make a number line) are both very useful. Use either to show your child that the numbers that have 6, 7, 8 or 9 as the units digit are closest to the next multiple of 10. Then point out that numbers that have 1, 2, 3 or 4 as the units digit will round down to the previous multiple of 10. Talk about numbers that have 5 as the units digit – it is normal to round up from these numbers.

Addition

As in Year 1, a number line is very useful for practising addition facts.

1 2 3 4 5 6 7 8 9 10 11 12 13 14 15 16 17 18 19 20

Keep asking questions such as: 7 + 5   8 + 2   4 + 3   9 + 6   8 + 5   7 + 6

Encourage your child to start from the larger number when counting on. For example, if they have to answer the question 3 + 7, help them to start with the 7 then make three jumps.

It is particularly important that your child knows the addition facts for every number up to 10:

1	2	3	4	5	6	7	8	9	10
0+1	0+2	0+3	0+4	0+5	0+6	0+7	0+8	0+9	0+10
1+0	2+0	3+0	4+0	5+0	6+0	7+0	8+0	9+0	10+0
	1+1	1+2	1+3	1+4	1+5	1+6	1+7	1+8	1+9
		2+1	3+1	4+1	5+1	6+1	7+1	8+1	9+1
			2+2	2+3	2+4	2+5	2+6	2+7	2+8
				3+2	4+2	5+2	6+2	7+2	8+2
					3+3	3+4	3+5	3+6	3+7
						4+3	5+3	6+3	7+3
							4+4	4+5	4+6
								5+4	6+4
									5+5

Your child will also need to know the addition facts for 20:

20	
0 + 20	20 + 0
1 + 19	19 + 1
2 + 18	18 + 2
3 + 17	17 + 3
4 + 16	16 + 4
5 + 15	15 + 5
6 + 14	14 + 6
7 + 13	13 + 7
8 + 12	12 + 8
9 + 11	11 + 9
10 + 10	

Informal written methods for addition

At school your child will be encouraged to start using 'informal written methods' to add together two two-digit numbers. For example:

37 + 26

This question can be approached in several ways but, as shown below, most teachers will use 'empty' number lines to do this. The teacher will write on the numbers they need and use arrows to show the process of adding on. The question 37 + 26 is likely to be completed in two possible ways:

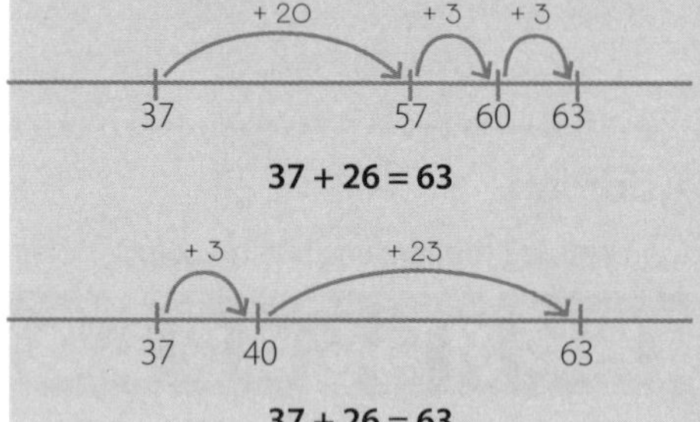

37 + 26 = 63

37 + 26 = 63

As you can see, both ways give the correct result.

Similarly, your child needs to know the addition facts for every multiple of 10 up to 100:

10	20	30	40	50	60	70	80	90	100
0 + 10	0 + 20	0 + 30	0 + 40	0 + 50	0 + 60	0 + 70	0 + 80	0 + 90	0 + 100
10 + 0	20 + 0	30 + 0	40 + 0	50 + 0	60 + 0	70 + 0	80 + 0	90 + 0	100 + 0
	10 + 10	10 + 20	10 + 30	10 + 40	10 + 50	10 + 60	10 + 70	10 + 80	10 + 90
		20 + 10	30 + 10	40 + 10	50 + 10	60 + 10	70 + 10	80 + 10	90 + 10
			20 + 20	20 + 30	20 + 40	20 + 50	20 + 60	20 + 70	20 + 80
				30 + 20	40 + 20	50 + 20	60 + 20	70 + 20	80 + 20
					30 + 30	30 + 40	30 + 50	30 + 60	30 + 70
						40 + 30	50 + 30	60 + 30	70 + 30
							40 + 40	40 + 50	40 + 60
								50 + 40	60 + 40
									50 + 50

This is not likely to be the method that you learnt at school but it is highly visual and logical! Try it at home with your child.

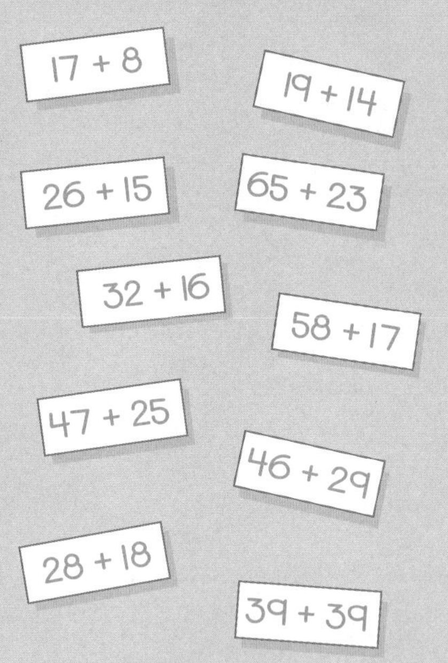

Subtraction

Carry on using practical equipment and the correct words as you practise subtracting with your child. Use your number line or hundred square again.

Help your child to learn the subtraction number facts for each number to at least ten: Write out the numbers 0 to 10 on small pieces of paper or blank cards. Show your child the number 10, then pick another number at random and ask, 'What's the difference between 10 and ...?' Keep picking random numbers and encouraging your child to find the answer as quickly as possible. After working on the tens, you could choose to find subtractions from 9 and so on.

10	9	8	7	6	5	4	3	2	1
10 - 0 = 10	9 - 0 = 9	8 - 0 = 8	7 - 0 = 7	6 - 0 = 6	5 - 0 = 5	4 - 0 = 4	3 - 0 = 3	2 - 0 = 2	1 - 0 = 1
10 - 1 = 9	9-1 = 8	8 - 1 = 7	7 - 1 = 6	6 - 1 = 5	5 - 1 = 4	4 - 1 = 3	3 - 1 = 2	2 - 1 = 1	1 - 1 = 0
10 - 2 = 8	9 - 2 = 7	8 - 2 = 6	7 - 2 = 5	6 - 2 = 4	5 - 2 = 3	4 - 2 = 2	3 - 2 = 1	2 - 2 = 0	
10 - 3 = 7	9 - 3 = 6	8 - 3 = 5	7 - 3 = 4	6 - 3 = 3	5 - 3 = 2	4 - 3 = 1	3 - 3 = 0		
10 - 4 = 6	9 - 4 = 5	8 - 4 = 4	7 - 4 = 3	6 - 4 = 2	5 - 4 = 1	4 - 4 = 0			
10 - 5 = 5	9 - 5 = 4	8 - 5 = 3	7 - 5 = 2	6 - 5 = 1	5 - 5 = 0				
10 - 6 = 4	9 - 6 = 3	8 - 6 = 2	7 - 6 = 1	6 - 6 = 0					
10 - 7 = 3	9 - 7 = 2	8 - 7 = 1	7 - 7 = 0						
10 - 8 = 2	9 - 8 = 1	8 - 8 = 0							
10 - 9 = 1	9 - 9 = 0								
10 - 10 = 0									

Informal written methods for subtraction

At school your child will start using 'informal written methods' to subtract one two-digit number from another. For example:

43 – 27

Again, the school is likely to use empty number lines.

The empty number line may be used for subtracting by counting back from the larger number to the smaller number:

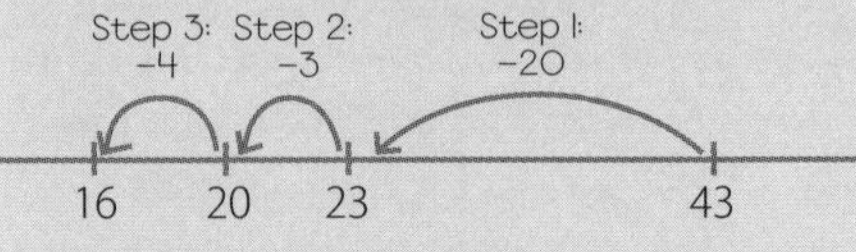

43 – 27 = 16

or

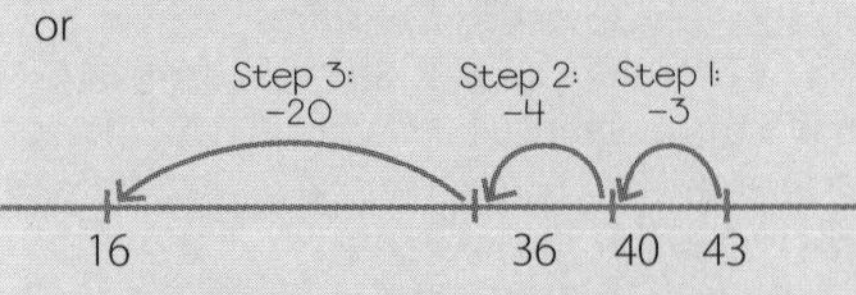

or

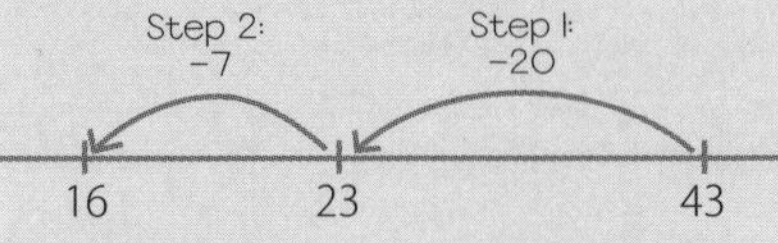

Or the empty number line may be used for counting up from the smaller number to the larger number:

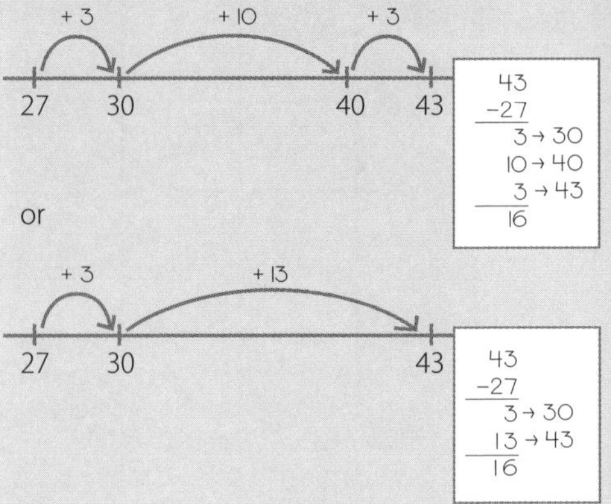

There are many ways that the empty number line can be used. Your child can choose what size 'jumps' to make to get from one number to the other.

Try asking your child to show you how they complete some questions.

34 – 18

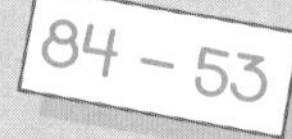

42 – 28

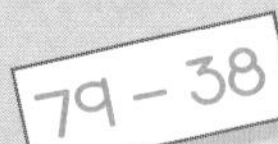

53 – 17

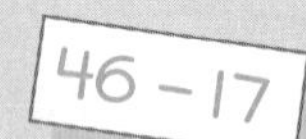

Multiplication

Practise the 2 times-table, the 5 times-table and the 10 times-table.

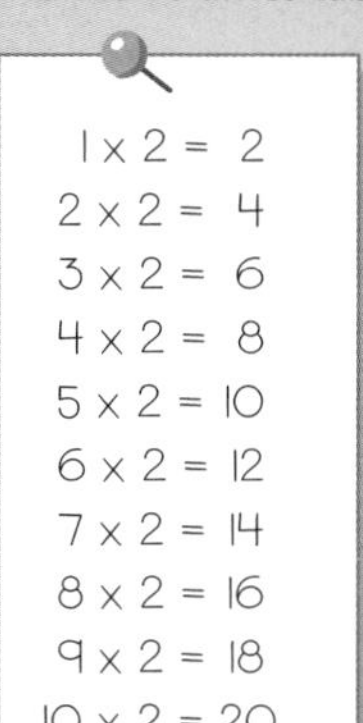
1 x 2 = 2
2 x 2 = 4
3 x 2 = 6
4 x 2 = 8
5 x 2 = 10
6 x 2 = 12
7 x 2 = 14
8 x 2 = 16
9 x 2 = 18
10 x 2 = 20

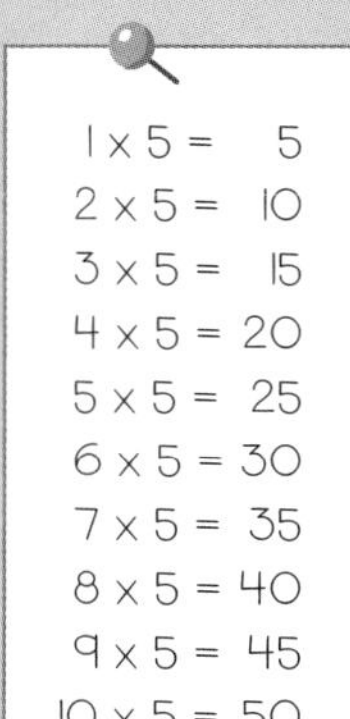
1 x 5 = 5
2 x 5 = 10
3 x 5 = 15
4 x 5 = 20
5 x 5 = 25
6 x 5 = 30
7 x 5 = 35
8 x 5 = 40
9 x 5 = 45
10 x 5 = 50

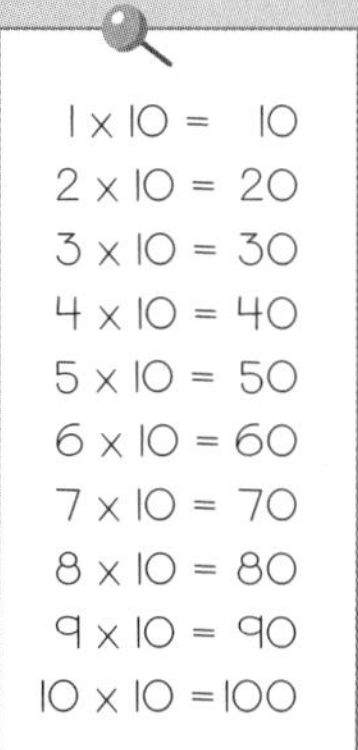
1 x 10 = 10
2 x 10 = 20
3 x 10 = 30
4 x 10 = 40
5 x 10 = 50
6 x 10 = 60
7 x 10 = 70
8 x 10 = 80
9 x 10 = 90
10 x 10 = 100

Try some practical multiplication activities. Both take off your socks and by using your fingers and toes you and your child can show the 5 times-table very effectively up to 8 x 5!

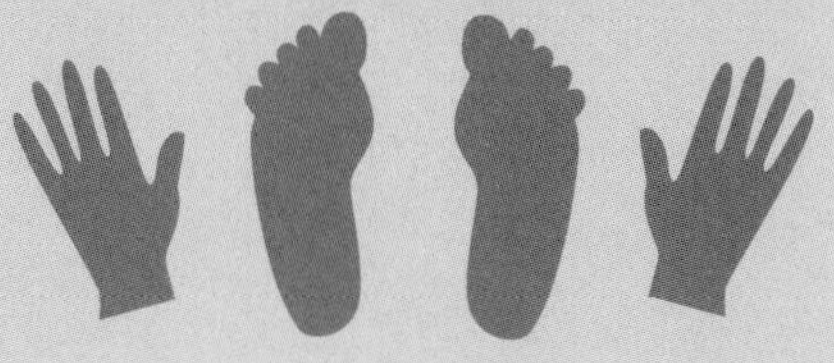

Division

Help your child to find division facts related to the multiplication tables.

For example:

3 x 2 = 6

so **6 ÷ 2 = 3**

and **6 ÷ 3 = 2**

The division facts are not normally written out as tables but the facts needed are as follows:

20 ÷ 2 = 10
18 ÷ 2 = 9
16 ÷ 2 = 8
14 ÷ 2 = 7
12 ÷ 2 = 6
10 ÷ 2 = 5
8 ÷ 2 = 4
6 ÷ 2 = 3
4 ÷ 2 = 2
2 ÷ 2 = 1

50 ÷ 5 = 10
45 ÷ 5 = 9
40 ÷ 5 = 8
35 ÷ 5 = 7
30 ÷ 5 = 6
25 ÷ 5 = 5
20 ÷ 5 = 4
15 ÷ 5 = 3
10 ÷ 5 = 2
5 ÷ 5 = 1

100 ÷ 10 = 10
90 ÷ 10 = 9
80 ÷ 10 = 8
70 ÷ 10 = 7
60 ÷ 10 = 6
50 ÷ 10 = 5
40 ÷ 10 = 4
30 ÷ 10 = 3
20 ÷ 10 = 2
10 ÷ 10 = 1

If possible try to use some realistic practical examples. Open a packet of sweets and work out how many you could have each if two of you share them out. Extend this by asking how many each person would have if there were five people. This could show up the problem of dealing with some that are left over, but note that the word 'remainder' is not normally introduced until Year 3.

Looking at shapes

In Year 2 your child will learn more about the 2-D (two-dimensional) shapes that they came across in Reception and Year 1. They will also be introduced to some new ones – the pentagon, hexagon and octagon.

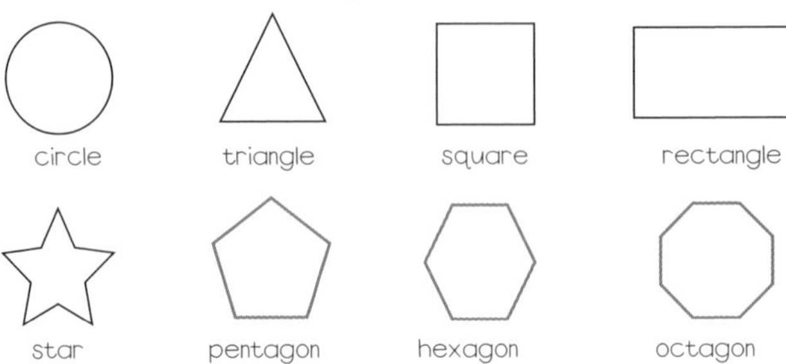

They will continue to learn about the following 3-D (three-dimensional) shapes:

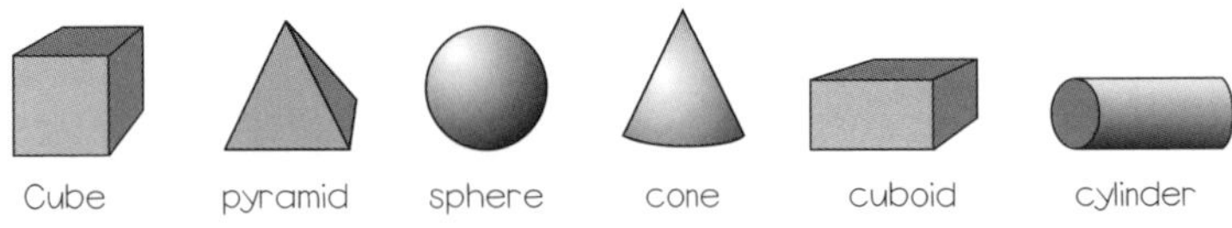

Talk about shapes asking questions such as:

- 'What shape is the front of this box?'
- 'What type of solid shape is the box?'

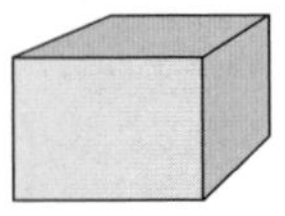

- 'What shape is the end of this tube?'
- 'What type of solid shape is the tube?'

Useful words

Use good vocabulary with your child, including words such as:

- shape
- flat
- curved
- straight
- solid
- corner
- face
- side
- edge
- end
- point
- surface
- symmetry
- symmetrical

At school your child will continue to learn about position, direction and movement. Help at home by finding opportunities to use words such as:

- over, under, underneath
- above, below, between
- top, bottom, side
- in front, behind
- front, back
- before, after
- middle, edge, corner
- left, right
- up, down
- higher, lower
- turn, whole turn, half turn
- clockwise
- anti-clockwise
- right angle

Measuring

Help your child to compare everyday objects:

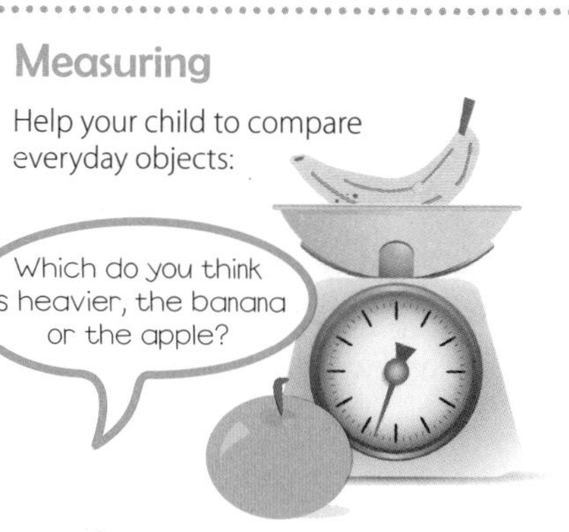

Ask them to weigh each item on the kitchen scales to see if their estimate was correct.

Ask your child to measure the string using a ruler. Help them to measure to the nearest centimetre.

Practise talking about time

Help your child to understand the concept of time by talking about the days of the week:

- 'What day is it today? What did we do today?'
- 'What day was it yesterday? What did we do yesterday?'
- 'What day will it be tomorrow? What would you like to do tomorrow?'
- 'Tell me the days of the week in order.'

Talk about the months as well:

- 'What month is it now?'
- 'What was last month?'
- 'What month will it be next?'
- 'In which month is your birthday?'
- 'Tell me the months of the year in order.'

Look through a calendar with your child, saying the months of the year as you go. Come back to this at different times but don't worry if your child doesn't remember the months of the year in order.

Talk about the seasons. Ask your child:

- 'What season is it now?'
- 'What is the weather like at this time of year?'
- 'Is it warm or cold?'

Help your child to tell the time for o'clock, half past, quarter past and quarter to.

Useful words

Use other time vocabulary whenever you can such as:

- morning
- afternoon
- evening
- night
- day
- week
- weekend
- birthday
- o'clock
- clock
- midnight
- half past
- hands
- seconds
- minutes
- hours

... and if your Year 2 child finds everything easy, have a look at what children are taught in Year 3.

Maths in Year 3

If your child is in Year 3 they will be expected to achieve targets for each aspect of mathematics. These are shown below, along with some quick and easy ways of helping your child with maths at home.

Using and applying mathematics

★ Solve problems involving numbers, money or measures.

Buy two or three differently priced chocolate bars. Ask your child questions about them: 'What's the total cost of all three? What's the change from £1 if we buy this one? Find the difference in price between these two. What's the change from £2 if we buy all three? How much would three of these cost?'

★ Represent information using numbers, images or diagrams.

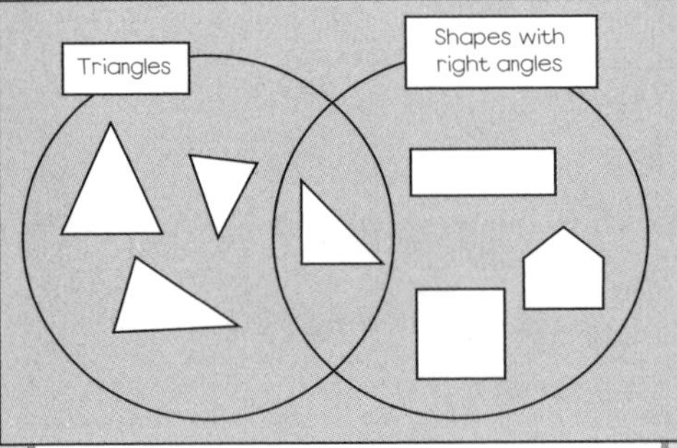

★ Follow a line of enquiry.

★ Make lists, tables and graphs to organize and interpret information.

★ Identify patterns and relationships involving numbers or shapes and use these to solve problems.

★ Describe and explain mathematical processes.

Counting and understanding numbers

★ Read and write numbers to at least 1000.

★ Write numbers in the correct places on a number line.

★ Partition three-digit numbers in different ways. For example, split the number 356

like this: **300 + 50 + 6**

Or this: **200 + 150 + 6**

Or this: **300 + 40 + 16**

★ Round two-digit numbers to the nearest 10.

Write a random selection of two-digit numbers on some blank cards. Ask your child to round them to the nearest 10.

When rounding numbers to the nearest 10, numbers such as 35 round up to 40 so 31, 32, 33 and 34 will round down to 30 and 35, 36, 37, 38 and 39 will round up to 40.

★ Round three-digit numbers to the nearest 100.

★ Identify fractions of shapes and write them correctly.

$\frac{4}{7}$ of the circle is shaded.

Knowing and using number facts

- ★ Know all the addition and subtraction facts for each number to 20.
- ★ Know the number pairs that total 100.
- ★ Know the 2 times-table, the 3 times-table, the 4 times-table, the 5 times-table, the 6 times-table and the 10 times-table as shown below.

1 x 2 = 2	1 x 3 = 3	1 x 4 = 4
2 x 2 = 4	2 x 3 = 6	2 x 4 = 8
3 x 2 = 6	3 x 3 = 9	3 x 4 = 12
4 x 2 = 8	4 x 3 = 12	4 x 4 = 16
5 x 2 = 10	5 x 3 = 15	5 x 4 = 20
6 x 2 = 12	6 x 3 = 18	6 x 4 = 24
7 x 2 = 14	7 x 3 = 21	7 x 4 = 28
8 x 2 = 16	8 x 3 = 24	8 x 4 = 32
9 x 2 = 18	9 x 3 = 27	9 x 4 = 36
10 x 2 = 20	10 x 3 = 30	10 x 4 = 40

1 x 5 = 5	1 x 6 = 6	1 x 10 = 10
2 x 5 = 10	2 x 6 = 12	2 x 10 = 20
3 x 5 = 15	3 x 6 = 18	3 x 10 = 30
4 x 5 = 20	4 x 6 = 24	4 x 10 = 40
5 x 5 = 25	5 x 6 = 30	5 x 10 = 50
6 x 5 = 30	6 x 6 = 36	6 x 10 = 60
7 x 5 = 35	7 x 6 = 42	7 x 10 = 70
8 x 5 = 40	8 x 6 = 48	8 x 10 = 80
9 x 5 = 45	9 x 6 = 54	9 x 10 = 90
10 x 5 = 50	10 x 6 = 60	10 x 10 = 100

- ★ Know the division facts that match the times-tables listed above.

Encourage your child to answer questions such as 24 ÷ 6 by referring to the 6 times-table. This will give them practice of their tables at the same time as learning division facts.

Calculating

★ Use mental arithmetic to add and subtract one-digit and two-digit numbers.

★ Develop written methods for adding and subtracting two-digit and three-digit numbers.

★ Multiply one-digit numbers and two-digit numbers by 10 or 100.

★ Use practical methods and informal written methods to multiply and divide two-digit numbers by one-digit numbers.

★ Find fractions of numbers or quantities.

Create some number flashcards by writing lots of different one-digit and two-digit numbers up to 30 on pieces of paper or card. Ask your child to pick two of the cards at random, then to find the total of the two numbers and the difference between them – a number line will help. Don't be surprised if your child is not quick at these activities, give lots of help and you will find that practice makes perfect!

Understanding shape

★ Relate 2-D (two-dimensional) and 3-D (three-dimensional) shapes to drawings of them.

★ Describe, draw and make shapes.

★ Use reflective symmetry.

Ask your child to look carefully at capital letters. Which ones have reflective symmetry? Place a small mirror on each letter – if the letter looks exactly the same in the mirror then it has reflective symmetry.

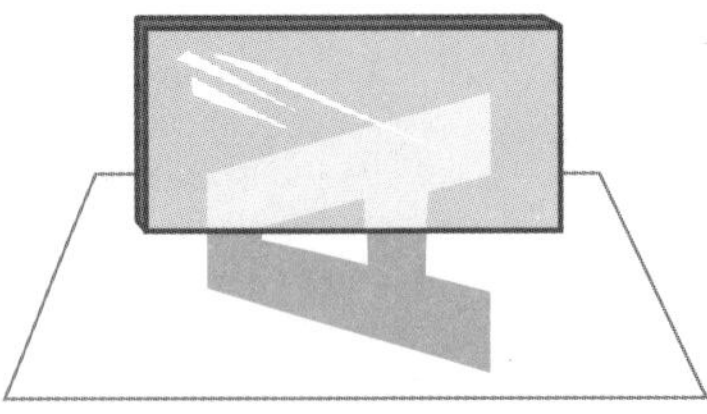

★ Use the four compass directions, North, South, West and East.

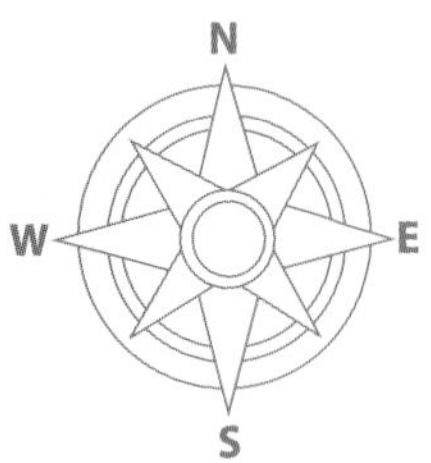

★ Draw right angles and compare other angles to a right angle.

Measuring

- ★ Know the relationships between:
  - kilometres and metres
  - metres and centimetres
  - kilograms and grams
  - litres and millilitres.
- ★ Use appropriate units to estimate and measure.
- ★ Read scales to the nearest division or half-division.
- ★ Read the time on a digital clock.
- ★ Tell the time to the nearest five minutes on an analogue (not digital) clock.
- ★ Calculate time intervals.

Handling data

- ★ Collect, organize and interpret data.
- ★ Use tally charts, tables, pictograms and bar charts (see page 17).
- ★ Use Venn diagrams and Carroll diagrams.

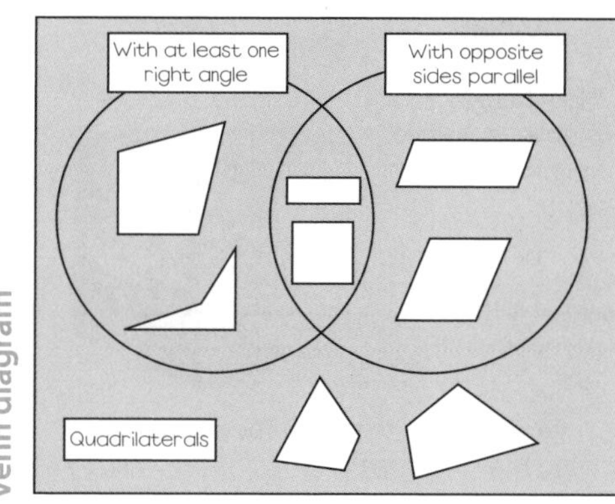

Venn diagram

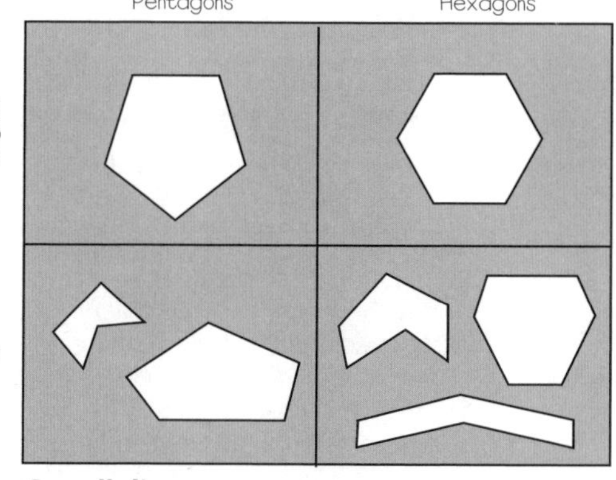

Carroll diagram

Venn diagram

In the Venn diagram above children have sorted a set of quadrilaterals according to whether they have right angles and whether they have opposite sides that are parallel.

Carroll diagram

The Carroll diagram has been used to sort a set of pentagons and hexagons.

How else can I help at home?

It's important to make maths as much fun as possible and to use lots of repetition. Talk to your child's class teacher to ensure that you know what your child should be practising.

Using and applying mathematics

Who's birthday?

Take every opportunity to talk about maths in everyday life. For example, discuss birthdays of family members and friends:

- 'Who's birthday is next?'
- 'What month is it in?'
- 'How many months is it until your birthday?'
- 'How many months is it since your last birthday?'
- 'What month is your birthday in?'
- 'What is the month before that?'

Encourage your child to look at the calendar, observing how it is organized.

Understanding numbers

Counting games

- Practise counting to one hundred and beyond.
- Practise counting in tens: 10, 20, 30 and so on to 100, then beyond 100 as your child becomes more confident.
- Practise counting back. Start with counting back from 10, then try counting back from 20 or 30. When your child is confident see how quickly they can count back from 100 on their own. Set the stop watch to see!
- Practise counting back in tens. Start with counting back from 100. If your child is confident try counting back from 200.

Activity ideas Number cards

Write some numbers on to pieces of card and help your child to read what they say.

365	292	418
942	600	789

Ask your child:

- 'Which is the biggest number?'
- 'Which is the smallest number?'
- 'Can you put the cards in order?'

Now give your child some blank cards and ask them to write these numbers on the cards:

823	516	180
75	999	245

Watch carefully to see what your child writes. For example, some children are likely to write 80023 for 'eight hundred and twenty-three' – if this is the case, explain that the position of each digit tells us whether it represents 'hundreds', 'tens' or 'units' (note that some schools use the term 'ones' instead of 'units').

Fraction fun

Use practical things around the house to explain fractions to your child. Cakes or pizzas or fruit such as apples or oranges are wonderful pieces of equipment for practising fractions! Talk about cutting them into equal pieces: halves, quarters, sixths or eighths.

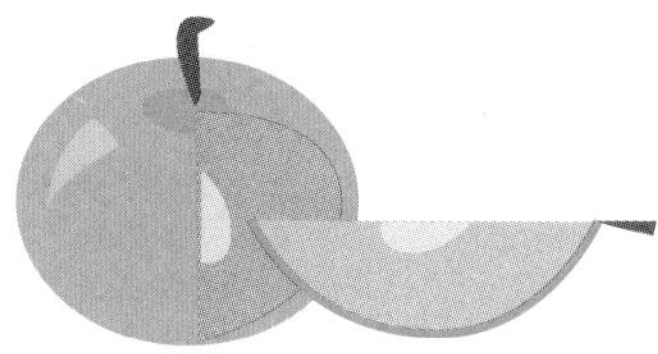

Adding and subtracting

Ask your child lots of questions such as:

- 'What's five add six?'
- 'Nine take away three?'
- 'How much do I have to add to 15 to make 20?'
- 'What's 20 take away 7?'

Don't be surprised if your child uses their fingers. They may also like to use a number line – that's fine too. With lots of practice they will suddenly begin to know the answers and won't need fingers or any other apparatus.

The important thing is for your child to have a strategy that works, without the use of a calculator or computer! When I asked a Year 3 child recently to add together six and five, he couldn't do it.

'How would you do this question if you were in school?' I asked. 'I'd type it into Google!' he replied, without hesitation. I tried it, of course, and it works but I hope that there are not many schools that are promoting this method as a viable strategy!

When your child is confident, ask some more difficult questions:

- 'What is 30 add 20?'
- 'Subtract 40 from 70.'
- 'How much do I have to add to 65 to make 100?'
- 'What's 100 minus 32?'

Activity ideas Number line

What you need

A number line showing the numbers 0 to 100

What to do

Lots of children find the questions above really difficult. Help them by using a number line. For example to answer the question, 'How much do I add to 65 to make 100?':

- ask your child to find the position of 65 on the number line
- ask them to say how far it is from 65 to the next 'tens number' – they should be able to see that it is 5 from 65 to 70;
- now ask how far it is from 70 to 100 – they should be able to see that there are three 'jumps' of 10 to get to 100, so that's 30;
- finally ask how far it is altogether from 65 to 100 – they should be able to say that it is 35.

Practise more addition and subtraction, this time asking questions such as:

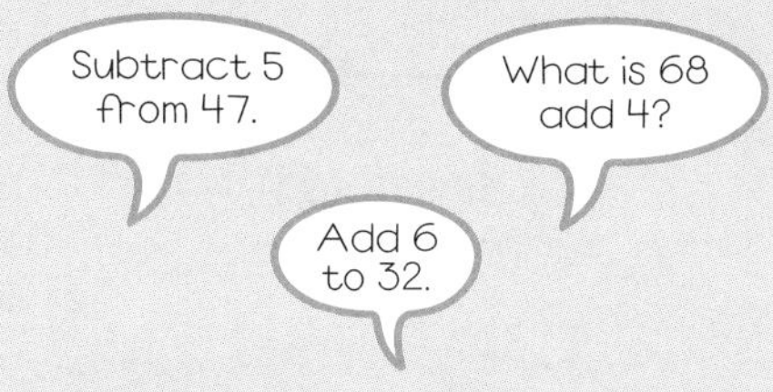

Your child can use the number line or fingers if they need to! This is fine so long as they know what to do and can get the correct answer.

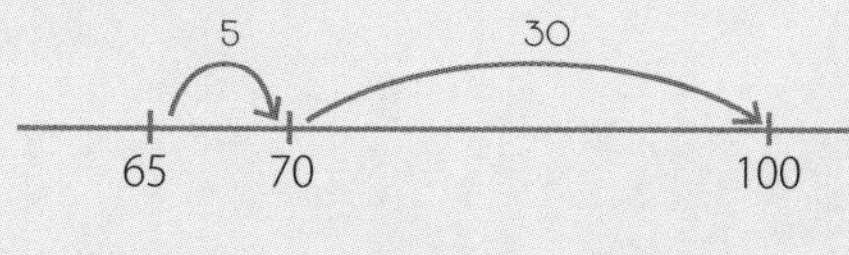

Written methods for addition

In Year 3 children are expected to 'develop and use written methods to record, support or explain addition and subtraction of two-digit and three-digit numbers'.

So, they will be expected to be able to work out a way of adding together two numbers such as 48 and 23.

You and I would immediately write these in columns. We would add the 3 units to the 8 units, put a 1 in the units answer and 'carry' a 1 to the tens. We would then add the 4, the 2 and the 1 that we carried and write 7 in the tens answer. Job done!

$$\begin{array}{r} 48 \\ 23 \\ \hline 71 \\ {\scriptstyle 1} \end{array} +$$

But don't be surprised when your child says: 'That's not how we do it in school.' Here are some of the ways your child may have been shown to add together two numbers:

Method 1: the empty number line

This is also shown in Year 2 on page 28.

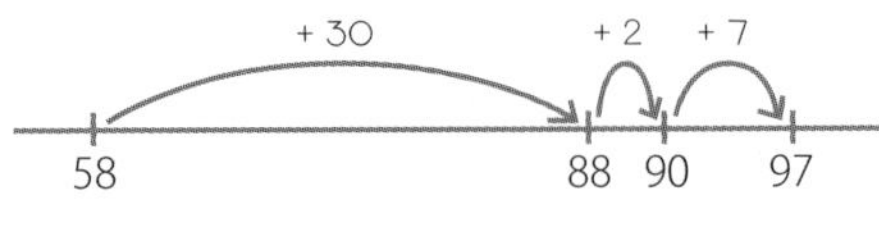

58 + 39 = 97

or

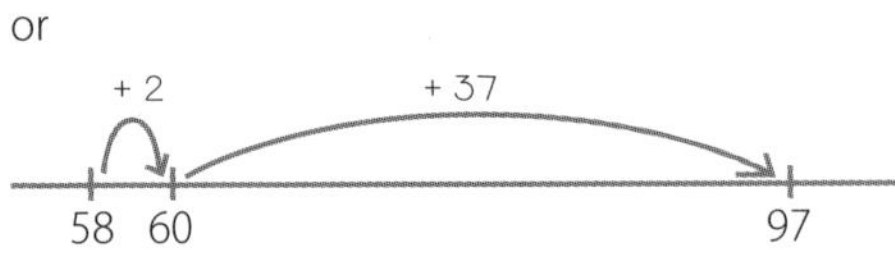

58 + 39 = 97

Method 2: partitioning

'Partitioning' means splitting numbers so that they can be easier to use when adding or subtracting.

In Year 3 your child may move on to using 'partitioning' like this:

58 + 39 = 50 + 30 + 8 + 9 = 80 + 17 = 97

Here you can see that the 58 and 39 have both been partitioned into tens and units so that the tens can be added separately to the units then the two results can be combined.

Sometimes the partitioning method is shown like this:

$$+\begin{array}{r} 58 \\ 39 \\ \hline \end{array} \quad = \quad \begin{array}{c} 50 + 8 \\ 30 + 9 \\ \hline 80 + 17 \end{array} = 97$$

Method 3: the expanded method

Some Year 3 children may move on to an expanded method in columns.

$$+\begin{array}{r} 58 \\ 39 \\ \hline 80 \\ 17 \\ \hline 97 \end{array} \quad \text{or} \quad +\begin{array}{r} 58 \\ 39 \\ \hline 17 \\ 80 \\ \hline 97 \end{array}$$

These methods can also be used with three-digit numbers.

Ask your child to show you how they answer questions like the ones below.

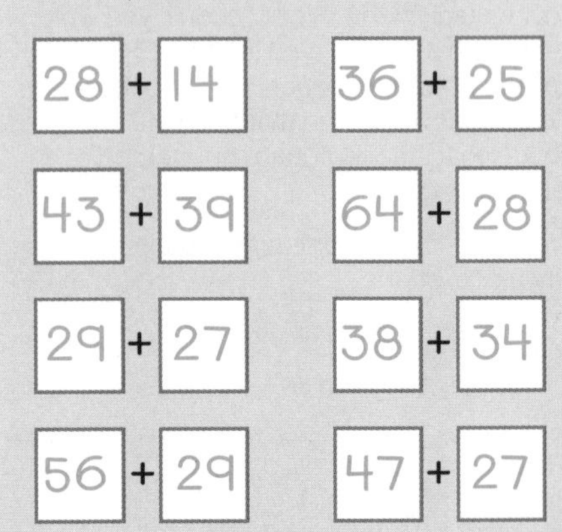

Written methods for subtraction

In Year 3 the children will be expected to be able to work out a way of subtracting a number such as 48 from a larger number such as 95.

95 – 48 = ?

Method 1: the empty number line

Again, the school is likely to use empty number lines. The empty number line may be used for subtracting by counting back from the larger number to the smaller number:

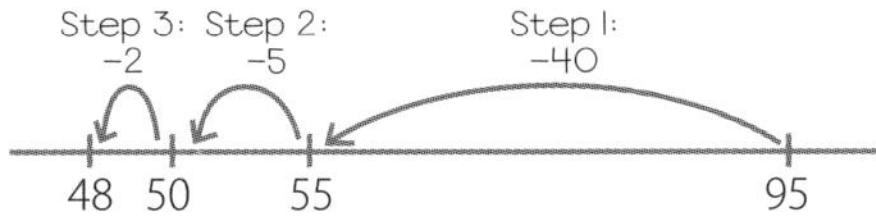

The empty number line may be used for taking away the smaller number from the larger number:

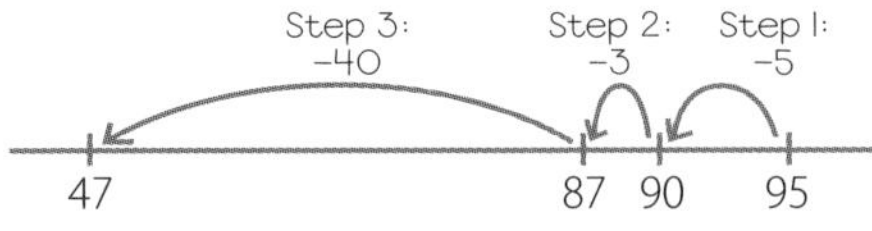

or

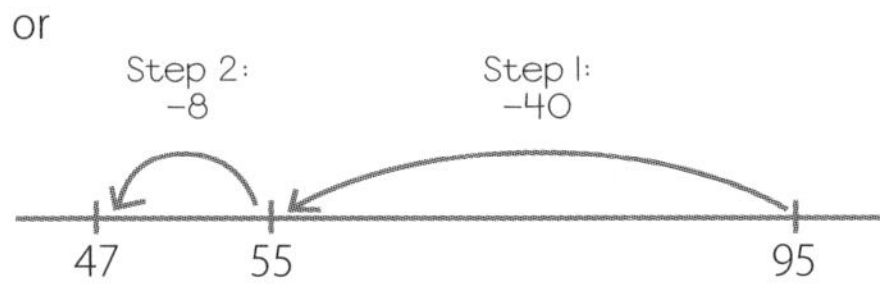

Or the empty number line may be used for counting up from the smaller number to the larger number.

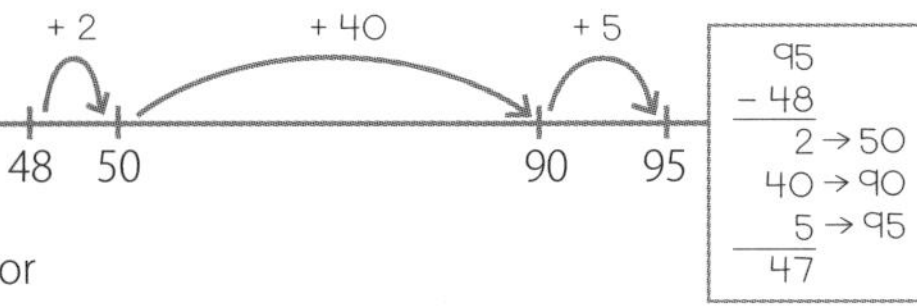

or

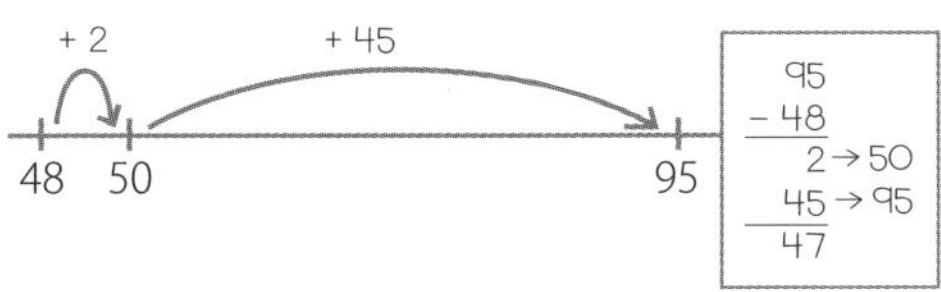

There are many ways that the empty number line can be used – your child can choose what size 'jumps' to make to get from one number to the other.

Method 2: partitioning

Your child may move on to 'partitioning' like this:

95 – 48 = 95 – 40 – 8 = 55 – 8 = 47

Your child may also be encouraged to partition like this:

95 – 48 =

90 + 5 – 40 – 8 =

80 + 15 – 40 – 8 =

40 + 7 = 47

Method 3: the expanded method

Although the last method looks crazy it does lead neatly to this expanded layout:

$$\begin{array}{r} 95 \\ -\ 48 \\ \hline \end{array} = \begin{array}{r} 90 + 5 \\ -\ 40 + 8 \\ \hline \end{array} = \begin{array}{r} 80 + 15 \\ -\ 40 + 8 \\ \hline 40 + 7 \end{array}$$

These methods can also be used with three-digit numbers.

Ask your child to show you how they answer questions like the ones below, using empty number lines or partitioning.

58 – 23 | 62 – 46

49 – 21 | 92 – 58

84 – 57 | 72 – 39

81 – 46 | 90 – 45

Multiplying and dividing

Practise the 2 times-table. Your child will already have learnt this in Year 2 but it is well worth practising again and again.

Ask your child to say it like this:

1 x 2 = 2	One two is two
2 x 2 = 4	Two twos are four
3 x 2 = 6	Three twos are six
4 x 2 = 8	Four twos are eight
5 x 2 = 10	Five twos are ten
6 x 2 = 12	Six twos are twelve
7 x 2 = 14	Seven twos are fourteen
8 x 2 = 16	Eight twos are sixteen
9 x 2 = 18	Nine twos are eighteen
10 x 2 = 20	Ten twos are twenty

To make the practice more interesting try timing your child to see how quickly they can say it!

Some people like to learn eleven twos and twelve twos as well – that's fine if you wish to. When your child is really good at repeating the table, ask them some random questions, such as:

'What's seven times two?'

Now remind them of the link between multiplication and division, by asking questions such as:

'What's 16 divided by 2?'

After practising the 2 times-table every day for a week, move on to the 3 times-table working in just the same way. Each week move on to a new table until you have worked together on the twos, threes, fours, fives, sixes and tens.

After learning the tables, you could start all over again with the twos. Don't be surprised if your child has forgotten the earlier tables that they appeared to know so well! It is not unusual for a child to be brilliant at the 4 times-table then to appear to forget it completely when working on the 6 times-table, for example.

But the human brain is a wonderful thing and the facts learnt early on are stored in there somewhere and will be even stronger when practised again. Eventually the number facts will be so ingrained that practice is no longer necessary and remembering them will just seem automatic to the child. Trust me, it works!

Looking at shapes

In Year 3 children will learn more about the 2-D (two-dimensional) shapes that they have come across in Key Stage 1. They will also be introduced to the semi-circle and the quadrilateral:

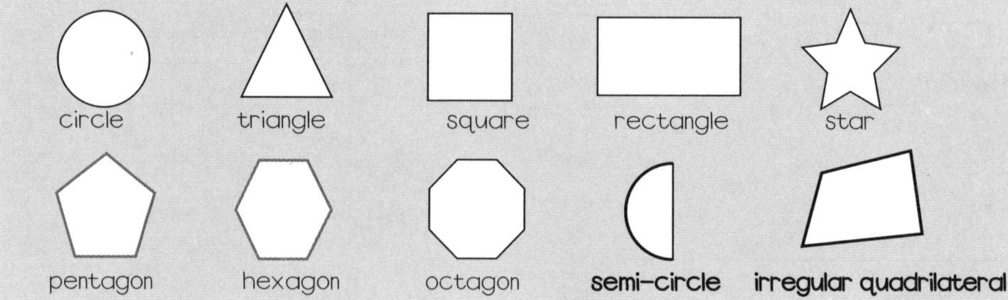

Explain to your child that the name quadrilateral is given to any four-sided shape, but squares and rectangles are special quadrilaterals. Ask your child:
'Do you know what makes them special?'

(Both of them have right angles at the corners. The square has four equal sides. The rectangle has two pairs of equal sides that are opposite to each other.)

Year 3 children will continue to learn about the 3-D (three-dimensional) shapes they met in Key Stage 1 but they will also find out about prisms and the hemi-sphere:

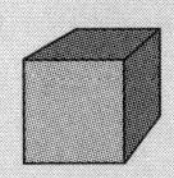

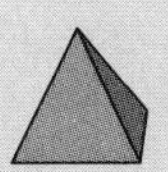

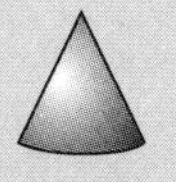

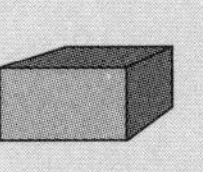

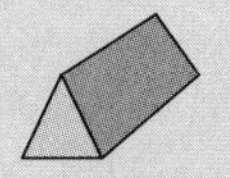

Talk to your child about shapes by asking questions such as:

- 'What shape is the end of this chocolate box?'
- 'What type of solid shape is the box?'

- 'What shape is the end of this tin?'
- 'What type of solid shape is the tin?'

Useful words

Use good vocabulary with your child, including words such as:

- shape
- flat
- curved
- straight
- solid
- corner
- face
- side
- edge
- end
- point
- surface
- symmetry
- symmetrical

At school your child will continue to learn about position, direction and movement. Help at home by finding as many opportunities as you can to use vocabulary such as:

- over, under, underneath
- above, below, between
- top, bottom, side
- in front, behind
- front, back
- before, after
- middle, edge, corner
- left, right
- up, down
- higher, lower
- turn, whole turn, half turn
- clockwise
- anti-clockwise
- right angle
- right-angled
- vertex (the corner of a shape)
- vertices (the plural of vertex)
- grid
- row, column
- angle

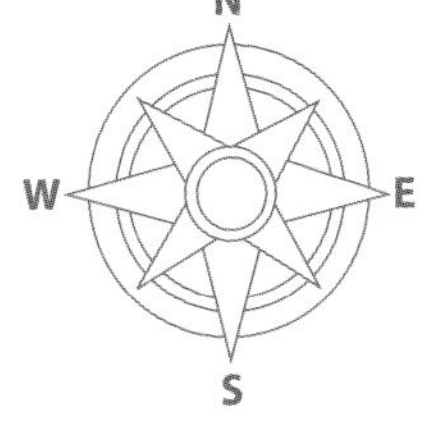

Weather forecast

Your child will be introduced to the four main compass directions.

Watch the weather forecast on the television and point out the North, South, East and West of the country. Ask your child:

'In which part of the country do you live?'

Measuring

Encourage your child to measure accurately using a ruler. Ask them, 'What is the length of each side of this triangle?'

Remind them to give the measurement in centimetres.

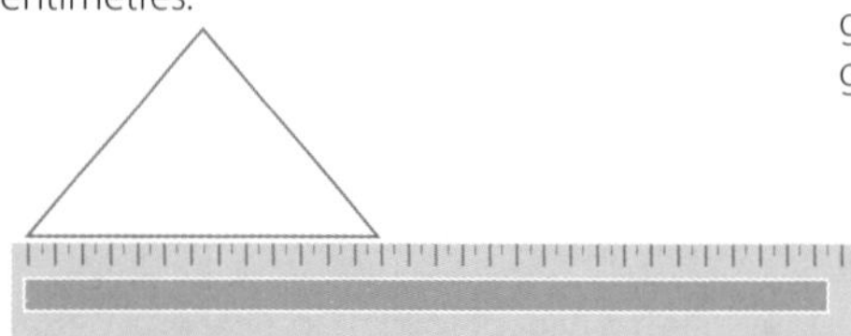

Ask your child to help weigh ingredients using kitchen scales. Remind them to give the weight in grams or kilograms.

Talking about time

Help your child to understand the concept of time by talking about the days of the week:

- 'What day is it today? What did we do today?'
- 'What day was it yesterday? What did we do yesterday?'
- 'What day will it be tomorrow? 'What would you like to do tomorrow?'
- 'Tell me the days of the week in order.'

Talk about the months as well:

- 'What month is it now?'
- 'What was last month?'
- 'What month will it be next?'
- 'In which month are we going on holiday?'
- Tell me the months of the year in order.

Talk about the seasons. Ask your child:

- 'What season is it now?'
- 'What is the weather like at this time of year?'
- 'Is it warm or cold?'

Help your child to tell the time accurately on a digital clock and to the nearest five minutes on an analogue (not digital) clock. Compare the times on the two clocks. When using an analogue clock, encourage your child to say 'am' for morning times and 'pm' for any times after 12 noon.

Useful words

Take every opportunity to use other words associated with 'time', such as:

- morning
- afternoon
- evening
- night
- day
- week
- month
- year
- weekend
- birthday
- o'clock
- clock
- midnight
- half past
- hands
- seconds
- minutes
- hours
- century
- calendar
- date

... and if your Year 3 child finds everything easy, have a look at what children are taught in Year 4.

Maths in Year 4

If your child is in Year 4 they will be expected to achieve targets for each aspect of mathematics. These are shown below, along with some quick and easy ways of helping your child with maths at home.

Using and applying mathematics

★ Solve one-step or two-step problems involving numbers, money or measures.

Buy three or four packets of sweets. A one-step problem could be 'What is the total cost of these?' A two-step problem could be 'Find the total cost of these, then the change from £5'.

★ Choose and carry out appropriate calculations, using a calculator if appropriate.

★ Represent information using numbers or diagrams.

★ Suggest and follow a line of enquiry.

★ Collect information then organize it and interpret it to find answers to a line of enquiry.

★ Identify patterns, relationships and properties of numbers or shapes and use these to solve problems.

★ Investigate a statement involving numbers and test it with examples.

★ Explain solutions to puzzles and problems out loud or in writing.

Counting and understanding numbers

★ Continue number sequences formed by adding a number repeatedly.

16 19 22 25 28 …

Tell your child a sequence of numbers such as '7, 9, 11, 13 …' Ask what number is being added to get from one number to the next then ask what would be the next three numbers. Move on to more difficult sequences such as '27, 31, 35, 39'.

★ Continue number sequences formed by subtracting a number repeatedly.

47 41 35 29 23 …

★ Use positive and negative numbers in context, for example, in relation to temperature.

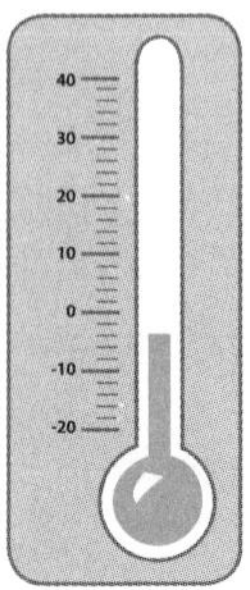

★ Write positive and negative numbers in the correct places on a number line.

★ Partition four-digit numbers in different ways. For example, split the number 2947

Like this: **2000 + 900 + 40 +7**

Or this: **2000 + 800 + 140 + 7**

Or this: **2000 + 900 + 30 + 17**

★ Round two-digit numbers to the nearest 10.

★ Round three-digit numbers to the nearest 100.

★ Round four-digit numbers to the nearest 1000.

★ Use decimal notation for tenths and hundredths. Relate this to money and measurement. Position decimals on a number line.

'Decimal notation' refers to how we write out decimals. For example the number 7.3 has 7 units (or 'ones') and 3 tenths and these are separated by a decimal point.

★ Know that:

$\frac{1}{2} = 0.5$ $\frac{1}{4} = 0.25$

$\frac{3}{4} = 0.75$ $\frac{1}{10} = 0.1$

$\frac{1}{100} = 0.01$

★ Identify equivalent fractions, such as $\frac{6}{8} = \frac{3}{4}$

Knowing and using number facts

- ★ Know all the addition and subtraction facts to be able to find the sums and differences of pairs of multiples of 10, 100 or 1000.

To pass the time when travelling, ask your child some quick questions such as '50 add 60', '90 add 40' and so on.

- ★ Know the 2, 3, 4, 5, 6, 7, 8, 9 and 10 times-tables.
- ★ Know the division facts that match the times-tables listed below.
- ★ Identify pairs of fractions that add up to 1.

1 × 7 = 7
2 × 7 = 14
3 × 7 = 21
4 × 7 = 28
5 × 7 = 35
6 × 7 = 42
7 × 7 = 49
8 × 7 = 56
9 × 7 = 63
10 × 7 = 70

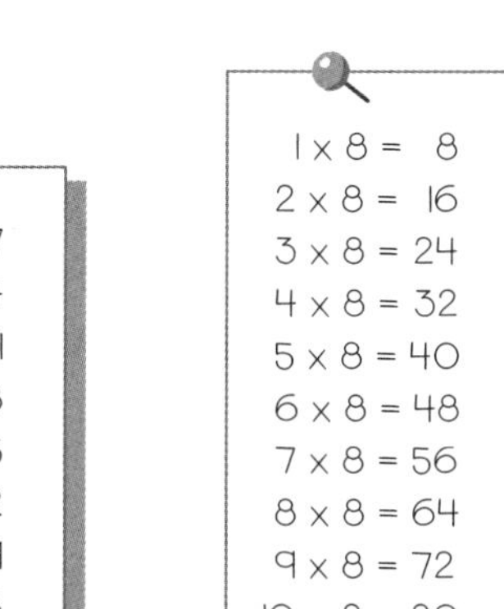

1 × 8 = 8
2 × 8 = 16
3 × 8 = 24
4 × 8 = 32
5 × 8 = 40
6 × 8 = 48
7 × 8 = 56
8 × 8 = 64
9 × 8 = 72
10 × 8 = 80

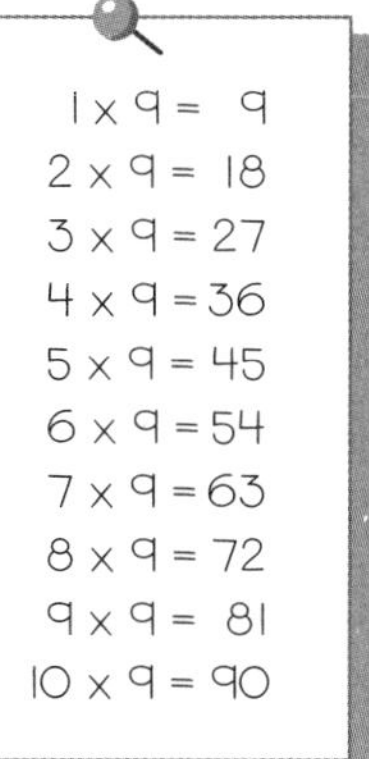

1 × 9 = 9
2 × 9 = 18
3 × 9 = 27
4 × 9 = 36
5 × 9 = 45
6 × 9 = 54
7 × 9 = 63
8 × 9 = 72
9 × 9 = 81
10 × 9 = 90

Calculating

- ★ Use mental arithmetic to add and subtract pairs of two-digit whole numbers.
- ★ Further develop written methods for addition and subtraction of two-digit and three-digit numbers.
- ★ Multiply numbers up to 1000 by 10 or 100.
- ★ Divide numbers up to 1000 by 10 or 100, where the answers are whole numbers.
- ★ Develop written methods to multiply and divide two-digit numbers by one-digit numbers. Find remainders when dividing.
- ★ Find fractions of numbers or quantities or shapes.
- ★ Use a calculator efficiently.

It's best to avoid saying 'just add zero' when multiplying by 10. Your child needs to see that multiplying by ten moves the digits of a number one place to the left. For example 37 x 10 = 370. The 3 was in the 'tens' position and has moved to the 'hundreds', the 7 was in the 'units' and has moved to the 'tens' and a zero has been written in the 'units' because there is always a digit in the units.

Understanding shape

- ★ Draw polygons and identify their properties.
- ★ Understand 2-D (two-dimensional) pictures of 3-D (three-dimensional) objects.
- ★ Recognise horizontal and vertical lines.
- ★ Use the eight compass directions:
- ★ Identify the position of a square on a grid of squares.
- ★ Know that angles are measured in degrees and that one whole turn is 360º.
- ★ Compare angles less than 180º.

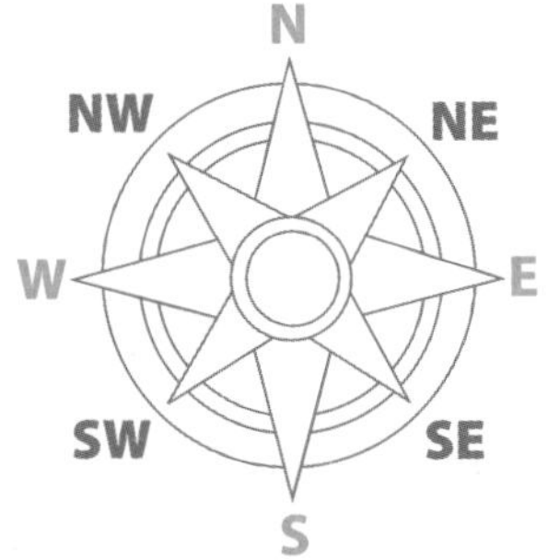

Look at a map of the UK together and ask your child to identify the North, South, West and East on the map. Then ask for the North-West, South-West and so on.

Measuring

★ Use appropriate units to estimate and measure.

Check that your child can measure accurately by giving them a ruler. Ask them to measure a line. Check that they start at the zero mark.

★ Know the meaning of 'kilo', 'centi' and 'milli'.

★ Use decimals to record measurements.

★ Read scales to the nearest tenth of a unit.

★ Draw rectangles and find their perimeters.

★ Find areas of rectangles by counting squares.

Talk about the perimeter being the distance all round the edge of the shape (like a perimeter fence) and the area as the amount of space enclosed by the fence.

Look at this example:

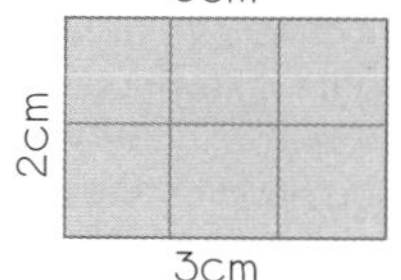

This shape has a perimeter of 10cm. It has an area of $6cm^2$.

★ Tell the time to the nearest minute on an analogue (not digital) clock.

★ Use am, pm and 12-hour clock notation.

★ Calculate time intervals from clocks and timetables.

Handling data

★ Decide what data to collect.

★ Collect, organize and interpret data.

★ Use tally charts, tables, pictograms and bar charts (see pages 17 and 37).

How we travel to school	
People who walk to school	𝍸 𝍸 II
People who come to school by car	𝍸 III
People who come to school by bus	𝍸 II

How we travel to school	
People who walk to school	12
People who come to school by car	8
People who come to school by bus	7

Tally chart
A tally chart may be used when gathering information as it's very easy to fill in the table.

Frequency table
The data from the tally chart can be transferred to a frequency table.

? How else can I help at home?

It's important to make maths as much fun as possible and to use lots of repetition. Talk to your child's class teacher to ensure that you know what your child should be practising.

Using and applying mathematics

Shopping maths

Help your child with 'using and applying mathematics' by taking every opportunity to talk about maths in everyday life. For example, when shopping talk about the quantities of each item that are needed to last the family for the week. Ask your child:

- 'How many cartons of milk are needed?'
- 'How much milk is in each carton?'
- 'What price is it per litre?' Look closely on the supermarket shelf to find the answer to this.

Understanding numbers

Car quiz

Make up some number sequences when travelling in the car. Ask your child to listen carefully then give a sequence such as:

2	4	6	8	?	?

and ask your child for the next two numbers.

Easy? Try this one:

42	39	36	33	?	?

Still easy? Try this one:

68	56	44	32	?	?

Remember that even the easy ones give practice in manipulating number.

Activity ideas Number cards

Write some numbers on to pieces of card and help your child to read what they say:

2495	3742	8615
7500	9200	4224

Ask your child:

- 'Which is the biggest number?'
- 'Which is the smallest number?
- 'Can you put the cards in order?'

Now give your child some blank cards and ask them to write these numbers on the cards:

1218	5000	4699
6328	2500	8750

Watch carefully to see what your child writes. For example, some children are likely to write 400060099 for 'four thousand, six hundred and ninety-nine'. If this is the case, explain that the position of each digit tells us whether it represents 'thousands', 'hundreds', 'tens' or 'units' (note that some schools use the term 'ones' instead of 'units').

Getting chilly

Look at an outdoor thermometer together. Does your child understand the readings on the thermometer?

Talk about differences in temperature. Explain that in the winter the temperature may go down to below zero. Compare a below zero temperature to the temperature today – unless, of course, today's temperature is below zero in which case compare it to a hot day!

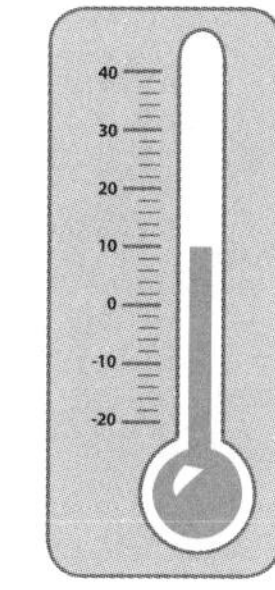

Rounding numbers

Ask your child to round each number to the nearest 10, 100 or 1000. This is surprisingly difficult.

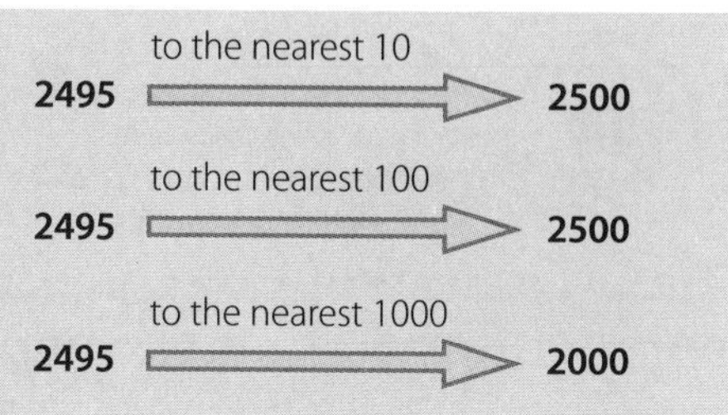

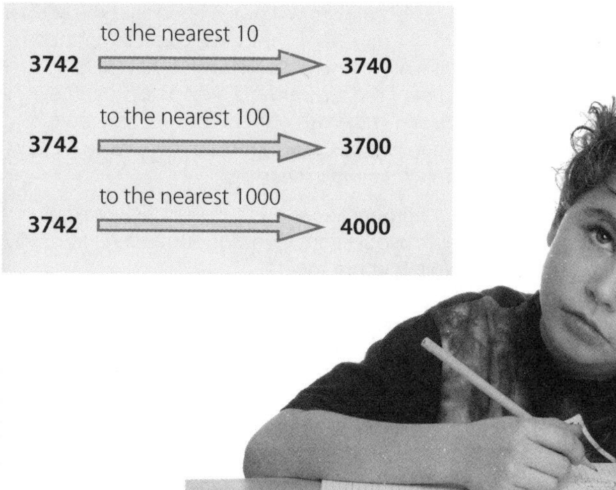

Fractions and decimals

Talk about relating familiar fractions to their decimal equivalents. Your child should know:

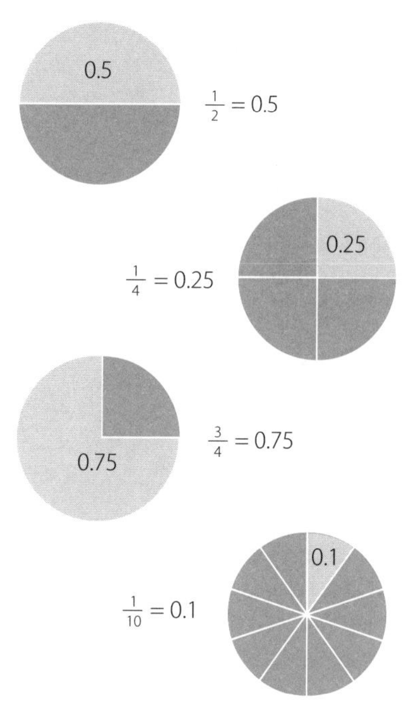

Adding and subtracting

It is essential that your child continues to practise addition and subtraction facts. Do this with your child as you travel to school in the car or wait at the bus stop. Ask questions such as '7 add 6' or '19 take away 8' – if your child finds these easy, that's very good news and you can encourage them to answer as quickly as possible. If your child finds this type of question difficult, keep practising and helping where necessary – practice really does make a difference.

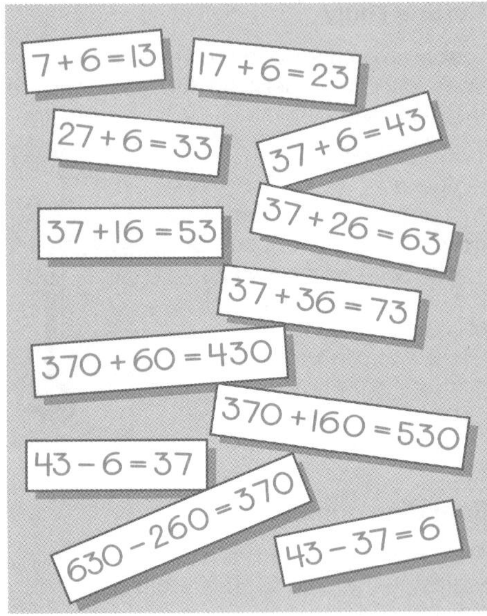

When you feel your child is confident with the addition and subtraction facts up to 20, move on to questions such as:

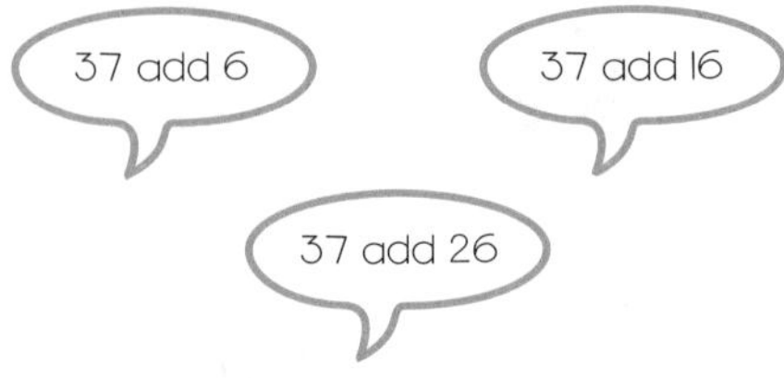

Encourage them to see that these questions are all related and each one will give an answer where the units digit is three.

Your child will become much more confident in maths if they can see the connections between different calculations.

Subtracting from 100

Many children make mistakes when subtracting from 100. This is well worth practising because we have to subtract from 100 when dealing with money or measurements.

Lots of children will give 43 pence as the answer to this question. They have correctly spotted that 60 is 40 less than 100 and that the units part of the answer will have to be 3 but they haven't taken account of the fact that more than 60p has been spent so there won't be as much as 40p in change.

A number line shows this very well. Make up lots of questions involving subtracting from 100 to talk about together.

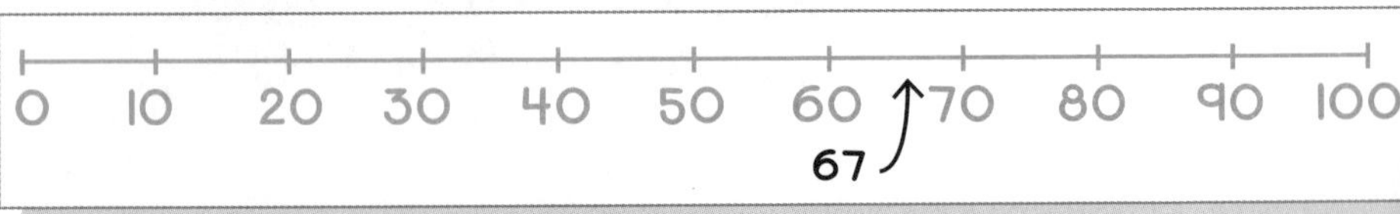

Written methods for addition

In Year 4 your child will be expected to 'further develop' written methods for addition and subtraction.

They will be expected to be able to work out a way of adding together two numbers such as 369 and 148. The methods that they may be encouraged to use in school do come as a bit of a shock when you are not used to them but they are logical when approached in a step-by-step manner.

Here are some of the methods your child may have been shown:

Method 1: the empty number line

This is also shown in Year 2 on page 30 and in Year 3 on page 41:

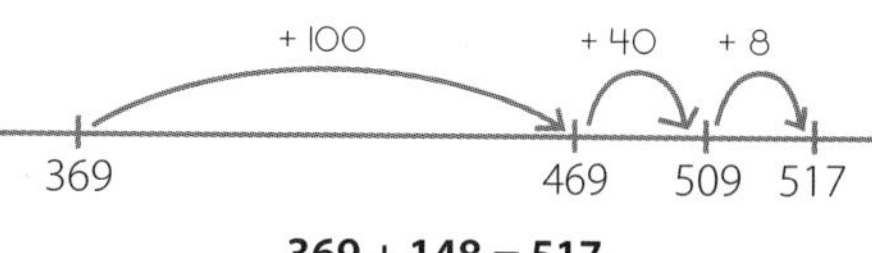

369 + 148 = 517

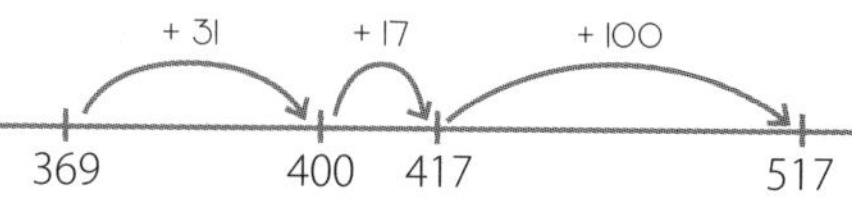

Method 2: partitioning

This is also shown in Year 3 on page 41:

369 + 148 =

300 + 100 + 60 +40 + 9 + 8 =

400 + 100 + 17 =

517

Sometimes the partitioning method is shown like this:

$$\begin{array}{r} 369 \\ +\ 148 \\ \hline \end{array} \quad = \quad \begin{array}{r} 300 + 60 + 9 \\ +\ 100 + 40 + 8 \\ \hline 400 + 100 + 17 \end{array} = 517$$

Method 3: the expanded method

Some Year 4 children may move on to an expanded method in columns. They may be encouraged to add the units first or the hundreds first.

$$\begin{array}{r} 369 \\ +\ 148 \\ \hline 400 \\ 100 \\ 17 \\ \hline 517 \end{array} \quad \text{or} \quad \begin{array}{r} 369 \\ +\ 148 \\ \hline 17 \\ 100 \\ 400 \\ \hline 517 \end{array}$$

Method 4: the column method

Some children will move on to the column method that we adults know and love!

$$\begin{array}{r} 369 \\ +\ 148 \\ \hline 517 \\ \hline {}_{1\,1} \end{array}$$

Ask your child to show you how they complete some questions, using empty number lines, partitioning, an expanded method in columns or the 'traditional' column method. It's a good idea to find out which of these methods the school uses, then encourage your child to use that method at home.

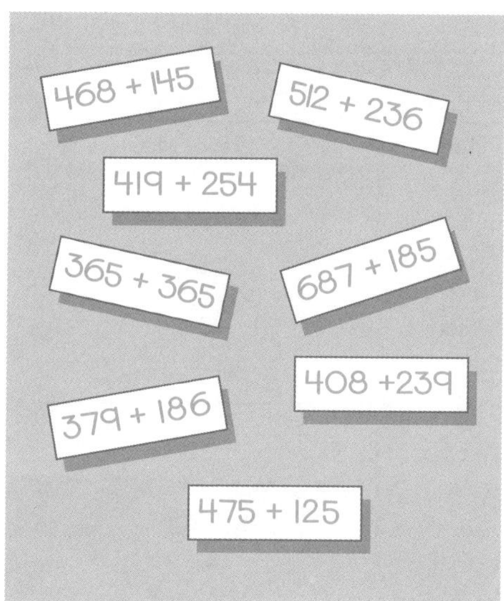

Written methods for subtraction

Following on from their work in Year 3 (see page 41), your child will be expected to be able to work out a way of subtracting a number such as 269 from a larger number such as 435.

435 – 269 = ?

There are, however, a bewildering range of methods that may be used for subtraction and it will be well worth discussing the method used in your child's school with their class teacher.

Method 1: the empty number line – counting back

The school may encourage the use of an empty number line for subtracting by counting back from the larger number to the smaller number:

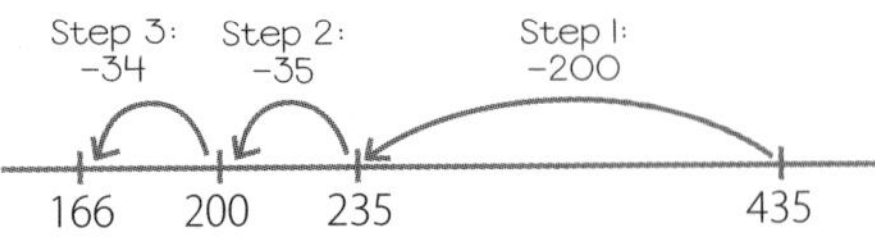

435 – 269 = 166

or

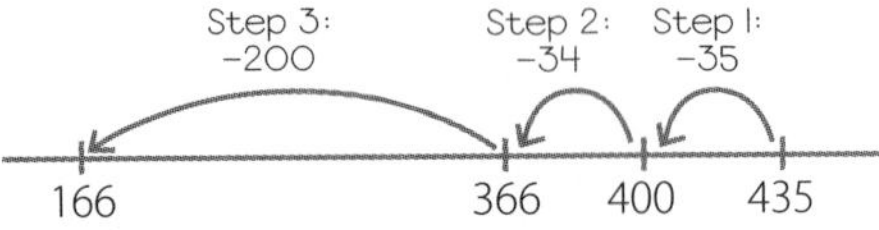

or

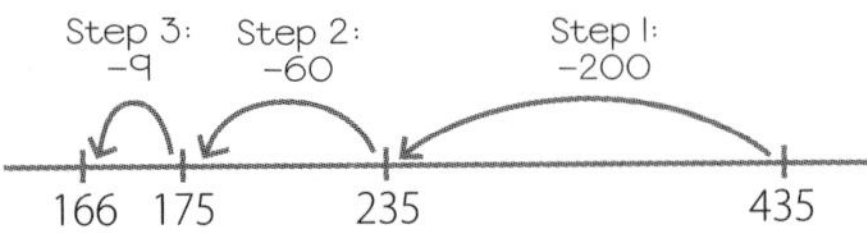

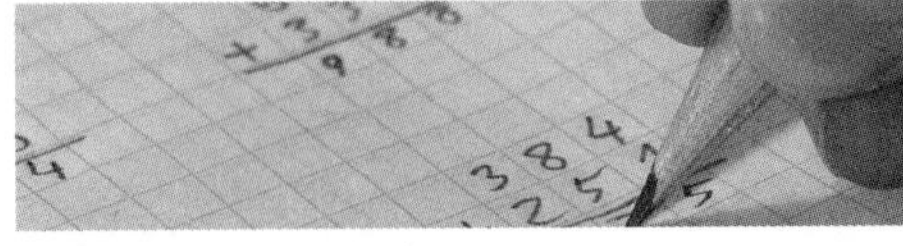

Method 2: the empty number line – counting up

Or the empty number line may be used for counting up from the smaller number to the larger number:

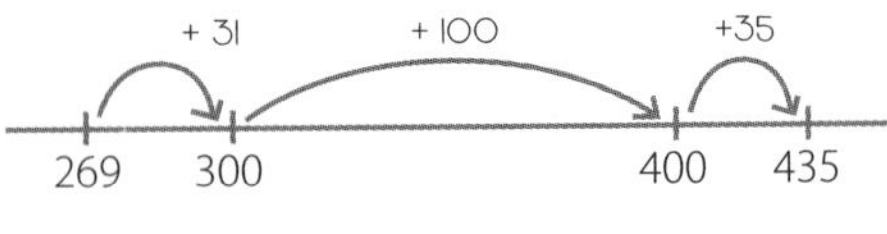


```
   435
 - 269
    31  → 300
   100  → 400
    35  → 435
   166
```

435 – 269 = 166

or

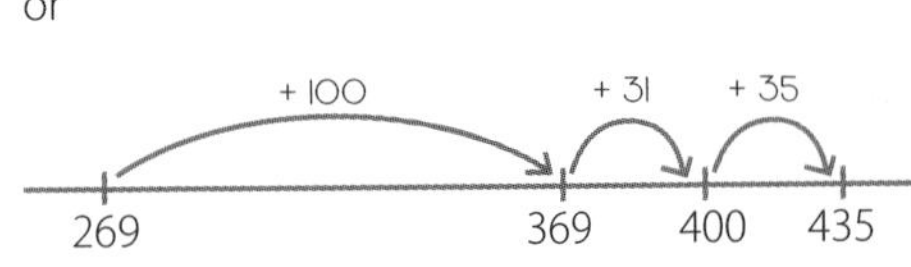


```
   435
 - 269
   100  → 369
    31  → 400
    35  → 435
   166
```

Notice the use of columns to record this process.

Method 3: partitioning

Your child may be encouraged to use partitioning.

You can look together at the partitioning process with these three different examples:

435 - 214, 435 - 243 and 435 - 269.

Example 1: 435 – 214

$$\begin{array}{r} 435 \\ -\underline{214} \end{array} \rightarrow \begin{array}{r} 400 + 30 + 5 \\ -\ \underline{200 + 10 + 4} \\ 200 + 20 + 1 \end{array} = 221$$

In this example your child should start with subtracting the units (some schools call these 'ones'), then subtract the tens, then the hundreds. Most schools will recommend that the children say '30 take away 10' rather than '3 take away 1', and '400 take away 200' rather than '4 take away 2'. The school may choose to move on from this method to the more traditional layout:

$$\begin{array}{r} 435 \\ -\ 214 \\ \hline 221 \end{array}$$

Example 2: 435 – 243

$$\begin{array}{r} 435 \\ -\underline{243} \end{array} \rightarrow \begin{array}{r} 400 + 30 + 5 \\ -\ \underline{200 + 40 + 3} \end{array} \rightarrow$$

$$\begin{array}{r} 300 + 130 + 5 \\ -\ 200 + 40 + 3 \\ \hline 100 + 90 + 2 \end{array} = 192$$

Here the child can see that the 400 + 30 has been partitioned to make 300 + 130 so that the subtraction of the four tens will be '130 take away 40'. Again, the school may choose to move on from this method to the more traditional layout:

$$\begin{array}{r} {}^{3}\not{4}{}^{1}35 \\ -\ \underline{243} \\ 192 \end{array}$$

Example 3: 435 – 269

Look at this example, where there are not enough units in 435 to subtract the 9 units in 269, and there are not enough tens in 435 to subtract the 60 in 269.

$$\begin{array}{r} 435 \\ -\ \underline{269} \end{array} \rightarrow \begin{array}{r} 400 + 30 + 5 \\ -\ \underline{200 + 60 + 9} \end{array} \rightarrow$$

$$\begin{array}{r} 300 + 120 + 15 \\ -\ 200 + 60 + 9 \\ \hline 100 + 60 + 6 \end{array} = 166$$

The 30 + 5 is partitioned into 20 + 15, then the 400 + 20 is partitioned into 300 + 120. This method leads to the more traditional layout:

$$\begin{array}{r} {}^{3}\not{4}\,{}^{12}\not{3}\,{}^{1}5 \\ -\ 269 \\ \hline 166 \end{array}$$

Ask your child to show you how they complete some questions, using empty number lines or partitioning. It's a good idea to find out which of these methods the school uses, then encourage your child to use that method at home.

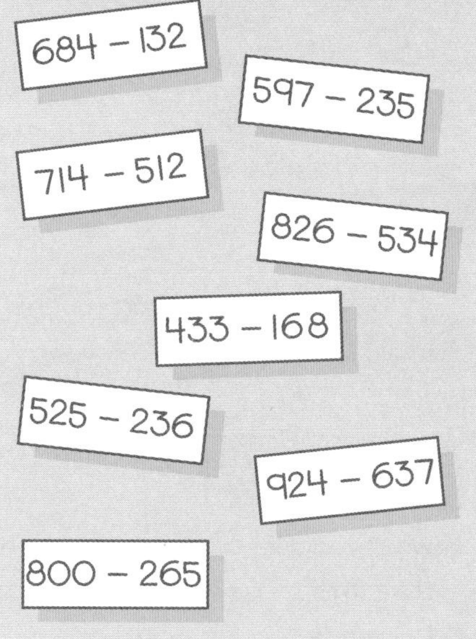

Multiplying and dividing

All eight to nine-year-olds will learn the time-tables up to 10 x 10. The school might call these the 'multiplication facts'. Many of us used to practise up to 12 x 12, mainly because 12 pence made a shilling and 12 inches make a foot, but learning the tables up to 10 is fine as long as your child really knows them.

So, help your eight or nine-year-old to learn the tables. Just work on one table each week, starting with the ones your child may know already, the twos, threes, fours, fives and tens, then moving on to the sixes, sevens, eights and nines. Ask your child's teacher which table the children are working on so that you can practise that one at home.

The best way to learn each table is to practise for a short time every day – just one minute is enough. For example, if practising the 4 times-table, encourage your child to say:

One four is four

Two fours are eight

Three fours are twelve

Four fours are sixteen

Five fours are twenty

Six fours are twenty-four

Seven fours are twenty-eight

Eight fours are thirty-two

Nine fours are thirty-six

Ten fours are forty.

Now ask your child lots of division questions, which make use of the tables. For example, you could ask:

- 'What's 28 divided by 4?'
- 'Share 36 apples between 9 people.'
- 'Divide 24 by 6.'

Written methods for multiplication

The methods they use in school these days are not the same as the ones that we learnt several years ago, but, if they're taught well, they are just as good and may be easier to learn. To help your child at home make sure that you are using the same method that is being taught at school. Ask your child's teacher to show you.

Here are some of the methods that the school may use for 56 x 4.

Method 1: informal recording

```
      56
  50  +  6
  ↓      ↓   x 4
 200  + 24  = 224
```

Method 2: the grid method

x	4
50	200
6	24
	224

Method 3: expanded short multiplication

```
  56
 x 4
 200     50 x 4 = 200
  24      6 x 4 =  24
 224
```

Method 4: short multiplication

$$\begin{array}{r} 56 \\ \times\ 4 \\ \hline 224 \\ \hline {}_{2} \end{array}$$

Some schools will show the children all the methods, starting with method 1 and working through each of them. Method 4 is the method that most of us were taught at school but many schools choose not to use this, encouraging the children to be really successful with method 2 or method 3. The school will have a 'Calculation Policy' and the class teacher should be able to tell you what this says in relation to multiplication.

Written methods for division

Many children and adults have an absolute fear of division!

Here are some of the methods that the school may use:

Mental division using partitioning.
Look at how we might partition 76 to divide it by 4:

$$76 \to 40 + 36 \xrightarrow{\div 4} 10 + 9 = 19$$

This method can also be used with questions that result in remainders. Look what happens when we divide 59 by 3:

$$59 \to 30 + 29 \xrightarrow{\div 3} 10 + 9\,r2 = 19\ r2$$

The partitioning method may be written out like this:

$$\begin{aligned} 76 \div 4 &= (40 + 36) \div 4 \\ &= (40 \div 4) + (36 \div 4) \\ &= 10 + 9 \\ &= 19 \end{aligned}$$

This can lead to a method of short division that looks rather unfamiliar to most adults:

$$4\overline{)40 + 36} \quad 10 + 9 = 19$$

This can be shortened to a much more familiar looking division

$$4\overline{)7{}^{3}6} \quad 19$$

Looking at shapes

Your child will learn more about the 2-D (two-dimensional) shapes that they have come across before, including learning some vocabulary in relation to circles:

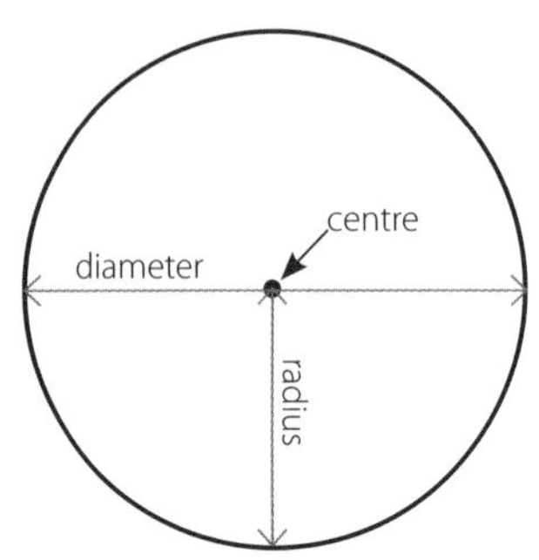

They will also be introduced to the equilateral and isosceles triangles:

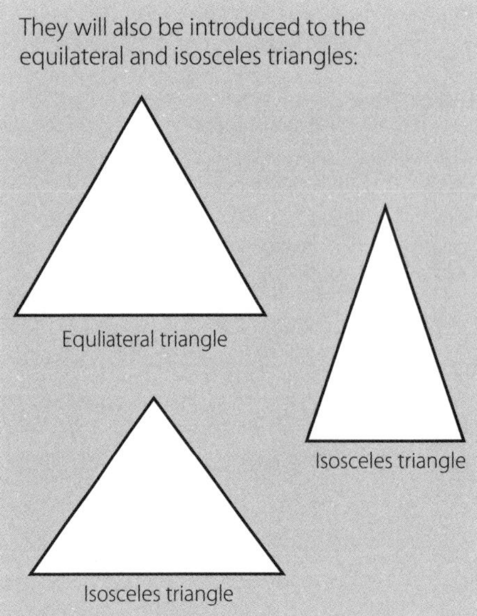

… and the heptagon:

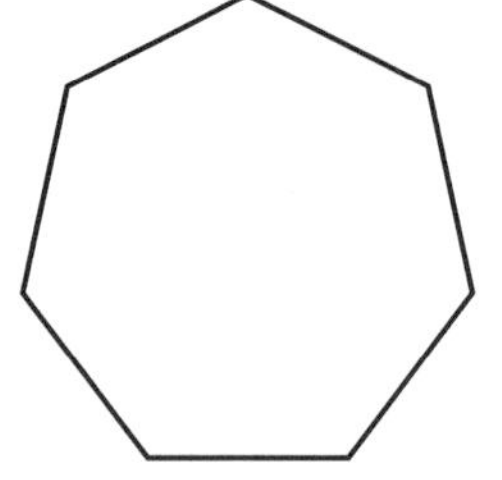

They will continue to learn about 3-D (three-dimensional) shapes, including the tetrahedron (triangular based pyramid):

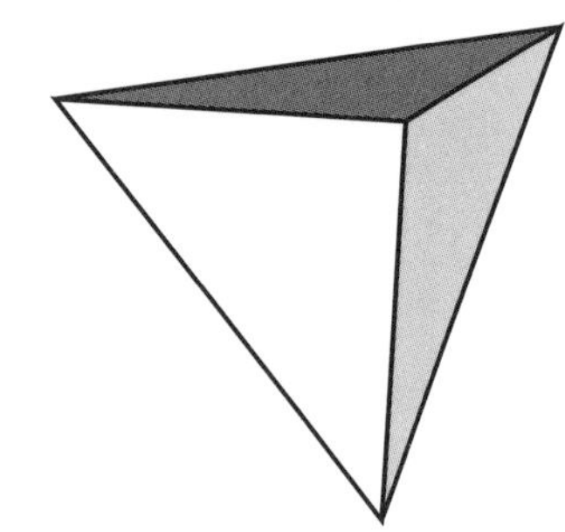

Your child will work with the eight compass directions. Try playing the 'Quick idea' game on page 48 .

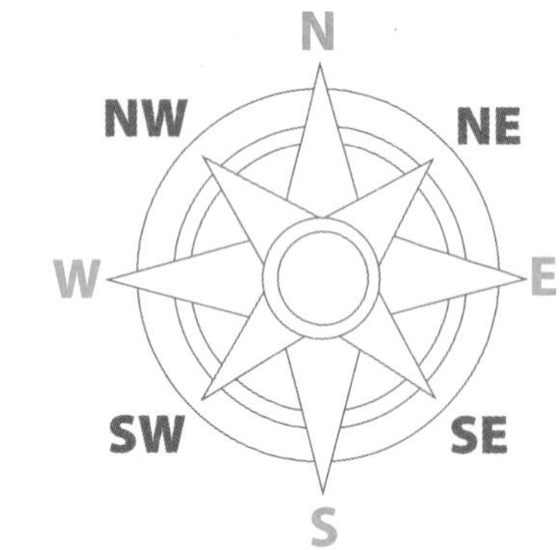

Measuring

Encourage your child to measure accurately using a ruler. Ask them, 'What is the length of each side of this rectangle?'

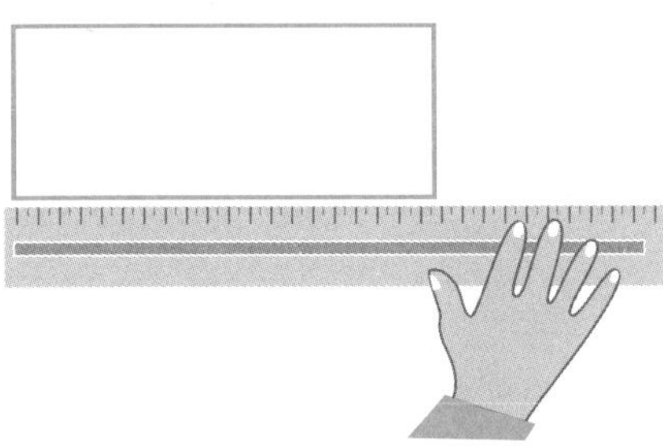

Remind them to give the measurement in centimetres. Now ask your child to work out the perimeter of the rectangle.

Ask your child to help to weigh ingredients using kitchen scales. Remind them to give the weight in grams or kilograms.

Encourage your child to interpret the recipe that you are using. For example, if the recipe suggests using 100 grams to make six small cakes, how many grams would be needed to make twelve of these cakes or nine of these cakes?

Talking about time

Reinforce the concept of 'time' with your child by asking questions such as:

- 'Tell me the days of the week in order'
- 'Tell me the months of the year in order'
- 'How many days are there in each month?'
- 'How many days are there in a year?'
- 'How many days are there in a leap year?'

Help your child to tell the time accurately on a digital clock and to the nearest minute on an analogue (not digital) clock. You could compare the times on the two clocks. When using an analogue clock, encourage your child to say 'am' for morning times and 'pm' for any times after 12 noon.

Useful words

Use other time vocabulary such as:

- morning
- afternoon
- evening
- night
- day
- week
- month
- year
- weekend
- birthday
- o'clock
- clock
- midnight
- half past
- hands
- seconds
- minutes
- hours
- century
- calendar
- date
- noon
- arrive
- depart

... and if your Year 4 child finds everything easy, have a look at what children are taught in Year 5.

Maths in Year 5

If your child is in Year 5 they will be expected to achieve targets for each aspect of mathematics. These are shown below, along with some quick and easy ways of helping your child with maths at home.

Using and applying mathematics

- ★ Solve one-step or two-step problems involving whole numbers and decimals for addition, subtraction, multiplication and division.

Dealing with money is an important everyday activity that is ideal for problem-solving. Ask your child how much you would have to pay to buy three boxes of tea-bags at £1.60 each – that's a one-step problem but if you ask how much change you would get from £10, you've turned it into a two-step problem.

- ★ Choose and carry out appropriate calculations, using a calculator if appropriate.
- ★ Find the information needed to solve a puzzle or problem.
- ★ Find possible solutions to a problem then confirm them in the correct context.
- ★ Plan and carry out an enquiry. Collect, organize and interpret information. Suggest further enquiries.
- ★ Explore patterns, properties and relationships involving numbers or shapes.
- ★ Explain reasoning out loud and use diagrams, graphs or text. Use appropriate images and symbols.

Counting and understanding numbers

- ★ Count on and back in whole number and decimal steps.
- ★ Use negative numbers when counting backwards beyond zero.

Ask your child to count backwards in threes from eight. They should say: 'eight, five, two, minus one, minus four, minus seven and so on'. Note that some schools will say 'negative one' instead of 'minus one'. If your child is finding any difficulty with this you could make or draw a number line like this:

Knowing and using number facts

★ Know all the addition and subtraction facts to be able to find the sums and differences of pairs of decimals. Find doubles and halves of decimals.

★ Know the 2, 3, 4, 5, 6, 7, 8, 9 and 10 times-tables.

★ Know the division facts that match the times-tables listed above.

It's always good to practise division so that your child is encouraged to use the multiplication tables. Ask questions such as 18 ÷ 2, 24 ÷ 8, 30 ÷ 6, 54 ÷ 9, and so on. If they find this difficult, allow them to refer to the times-tables.

★ Multiply pairs of multiples of 10 and 100. Find the corresponding division facts.

★ Identify pairs of factors of two-digit whole numbers.

★ Find common multiples.

1 x 2 = 2
2 x 2 = 4
3 x 2 = 6
4 x 2 = 8
5 x 2 = 10
6 x 2 = 12
7 x 2 = 14
8 x 2 = 16
9 x 2 = 18
10 x 2 = 20

1 x 3 = 3
2 x 3 = 6
3 x 3 = 9
4 x 3 = 12
5 x 3 = 15
6 x 3 = 18
7 x 3 = 21
8 x 3 = 24
9 x 3 = 27
10 x 3 = 30

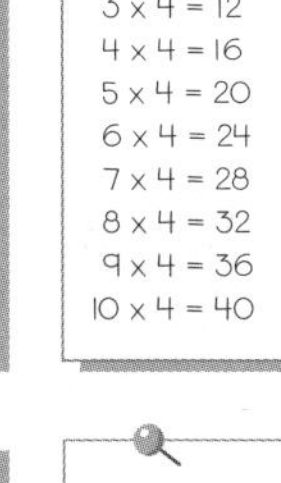

1 x 4 = 4
2 x 4 = 8
3 x 4 = 12
4 x 4 = 16
5 x 4 = 20
6 x 4 = 24
7 x 4 = 28
8 x 4 = 32
9 x 4 = 36
10 x 4 = 40

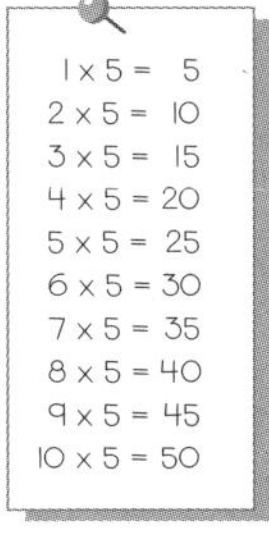

1 x 5 = 5
2 x 5 = 10
3 x 5 = 15
4 x 5 = 20
5 x 5 = 25
6 x 5 = 30
7 x 5 = 35
8 x 5 = 40
9 x 5 = 45
10 x 5 = 50

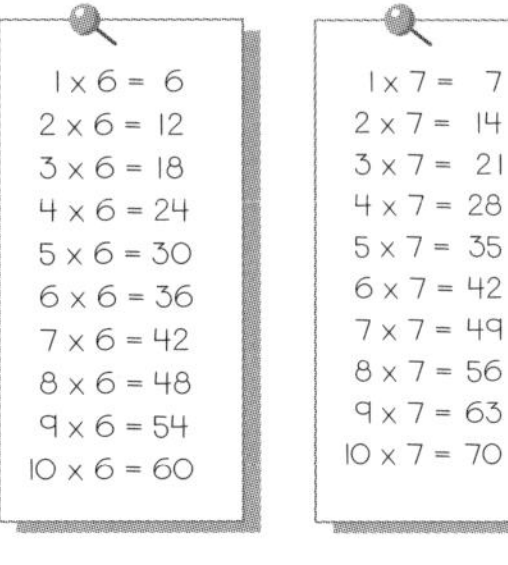

1 x 6 = 6
2 x 6 = 12
3 x 6 = 18
4 x 6 = 24
5 x 6 = 30
6 x 6 = 36
7 x 6 = 42
8 x 6 = 48
9 x 6 = 54
10 x 6 = 60

1 x 7 = 7
2 x 7 = 14
3 x 7 = 21
4 x 7 = 28
5 x 7 = 35
6 x 7 = 42
7 x 7 = 49
8 x 7 = 56
9 x 7 = 63
10 x 7 = 70

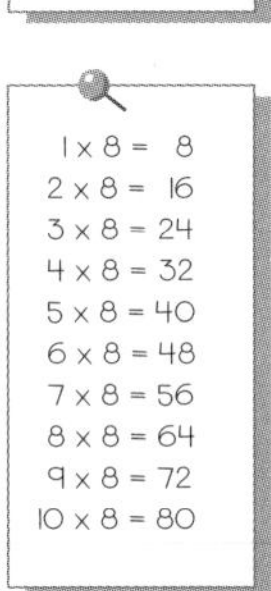

1 x 8 = 8
2 x 8 = 16
3 x 8 = 24
4 x 8 = 32
5 x 8 = 40
6 x 8 = 48
7 x 8 = 56
8 x 8 = 64
9 x 8 = 72
10 x 8 = 80

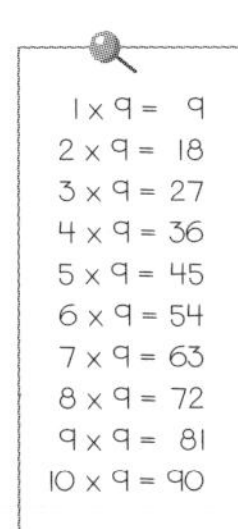

1 x 9 = 9
2 x 9 = 18
3 x 9 = 27
4 x 9 = 36
5 x 9 = 45
6 x 9 = 54
7 x 9 = 63
8 x 9 = 72
9 x 9 = 81
10 x 9 = 90

1 x 10 = 10
2 x 10 = 20
3 x 10 = 30
4 x 10 = 40
5 x 10 = 50
6 x 10 = 60
7 x 10 = 70
8 x 10 = 80
9 x 10 = 90
10 x 10 = 100

★ Relate whole numbers and decimals to their positions on a number line.

−3 −2 −1 0 1 2 3 4 5

−1.7 2.4

★ Explain what each digit means in whole numbers and decimals with up to two places. Round these numbers. Put these numbers in order.

★ Express one number as a fraction of another one – for example, say that two out of three is $\frac{2}{3}$.

★ Find equivalent fractions.

★ Relate fractions to decimals.

★ Show tenths and hundredths as percentages.

Calculating

★ Use mental arithmetic for a range of whole-number calculations.

Practise subtracting from 100, asking questions such as 'take 27 from 100'. Many children make mistakes with this type of question, giving the answer 83 instead of the correct one, 73. Using a number line can help.

★ Use efficient written methods for addition and subtraction.

★ Add and subtract whole numbers and decimals with up to two places.

★ Multiply and divide whole numbers and decimals by 10, 100 or 1000.

★ Use efficient written methods for multiplication and division.

★ Find fractions of numbers or quantities or shapes by using division.

★ Find percentages of numbers and quantities.

★ Use a calculator efficiently.

Understanding shape

★ Draw 2-D shapes using knowledge of their properties.

★ Draw nets of 3-D shapes.

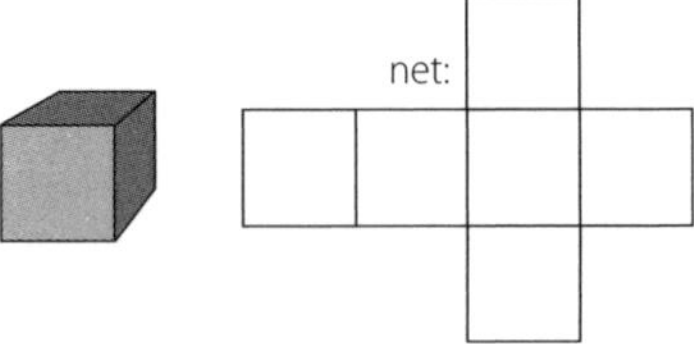

★ Use coordinates in the first quadrant.

The 'first quadrant' means the part of the graph above the x-axis and to the right of the y-axis. Look at the diagram:

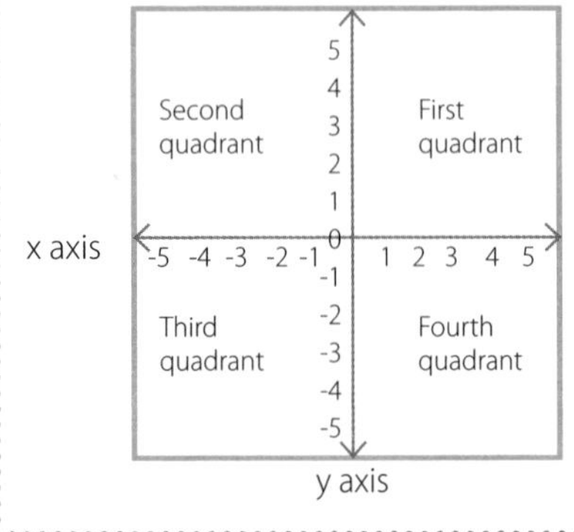

★ Recognise parallel lines.

parallel lines

★ Recognise perpendicular lines.

perpendicular lines

★ Use a set-square and a ruler to draw shapes.

★ Use symmetry to complete patterns or reflections.

★ Identify acute and obtuse angles. Estimate the sizes of acute and obtuse angles. Measure them or draw them using an angle measurer or a protractor.

handy tip

Acute angles are angles smaller than a right angle, that is, smaller than 90°.

Obtuse angles are bigger than 90° but smaller than 180°.

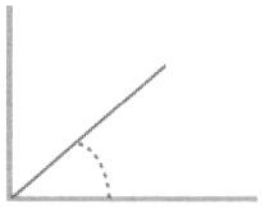

Acute angle

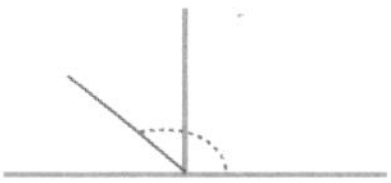

Obtuse angle

★ Calculate angles in a straight line.

Draw some straight lines each with another line meeting them at an angle. Draw on one of the angles made then ask your child to calculate the size of the other angle by subtracting from 180.

Measuring

- ★ Use appropriate units to estimate and measure.
- ★ Convert larger to smaller units, for example, convert 1.6 metres to 160 centimetres or to 1600 millimetres.
- ★ Interpret scales on measuring instruments, including where a reading lies between two unnumbered divisions.
- ★ Draw and measure lines to the nearest millimetre.
- ★ Measure the sides of polygons then add these to find the perimeters.

A polygon is a flat shape with at least three sides. For example, a hexagon is a polygon with six sides.

- ★ Find the area of a rectangle by multiplying the length by the width.
- ★ Understand the 24-hour clock notation and use this to interpret timetables.
- ★ Find time intervals using a calendar.

Handling data

- Discuss events using vocabulary related to chance or likelihood.
- Collect data and organize it to answer a set of related questions.
- Draw frequency tables, pictograms, bar graphs and line graphs.
- Find the mode of a set of data and explain what it shows.

The mode is the piece of data that appears most often. For example, your child has a modal score of 9 if they get the following scores in the weekly spelling tests: 9 10 7 9 10 8 9 8

Tally chart

How we travel to school	
People who walk to school	𝍸 𝍸 II
People who come to school by car	𝍸 III
People who come to school by bus	𝍸 II

Bar graph

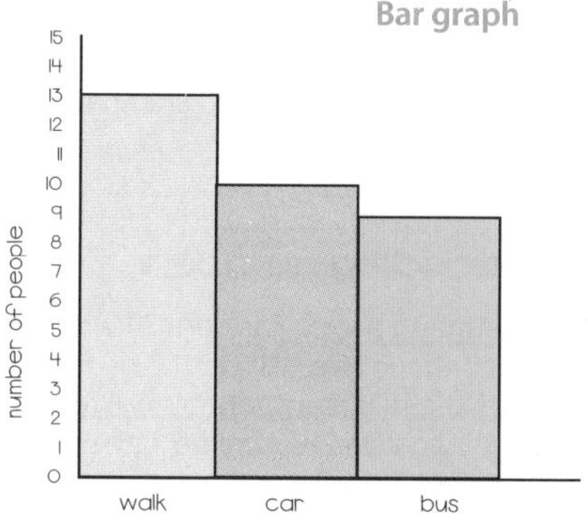

Frequency table

How we travel to school	
People who walk to school	12
People who come to school by car	8
People who come to school by bus	7

Pictogram

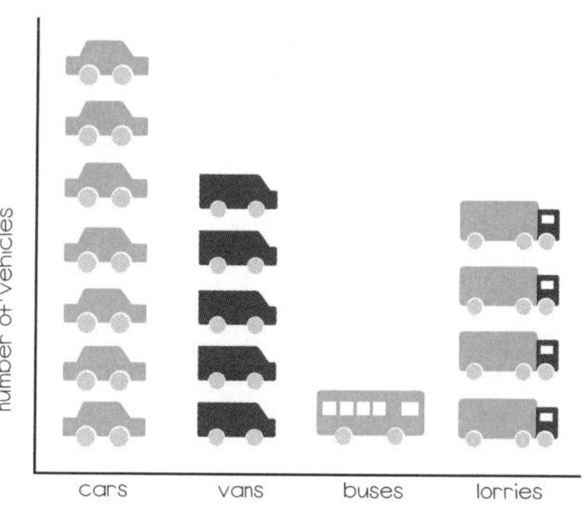

Line graph

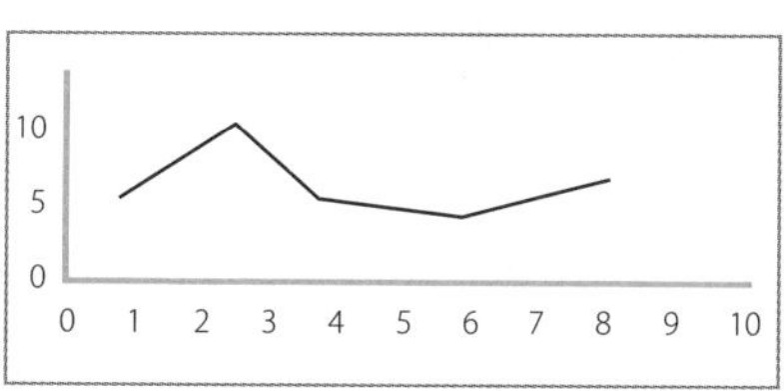

? How else can I help at home?

It's important to make maths as much fun as possible and to use lots of repetition. Talk to your child's class teacher to ensure that you know what your child should be practising.

Using and applying mathematics

On a journey

To encourage your child in 'using and applying mathematics' try to take every opportunity to talk about maths in everyday life. For example, when going on a long journey talk about how far it is in miles and how long it's likely to take. Note that children in school will be taught mainly about kilometres instead of miles. Discuss how far you've travelled after half an hour, an hour and so on. Ask:

- 'How far is there left to go?'
- 'How long will that take?'
- 'What speed are we currently travelling at?'
- 'How many minutes did we spend at the services?'

Understanding numbers

Practise counting backwards from 20 with your child, but continue beyond 0 to the negative numbers. Note that many schools will refer to 'negative 1', 'negative 2,' and so on, rather than 'minus 1', 'minus 2' and so on.

Talk about relating familiar fractions to their decimal equivalents. Your child should know:

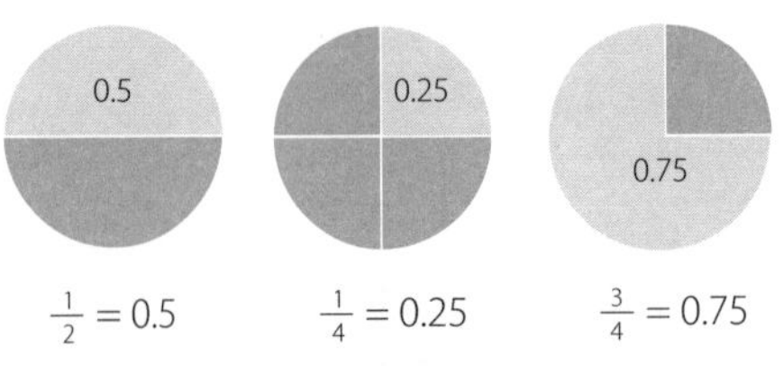

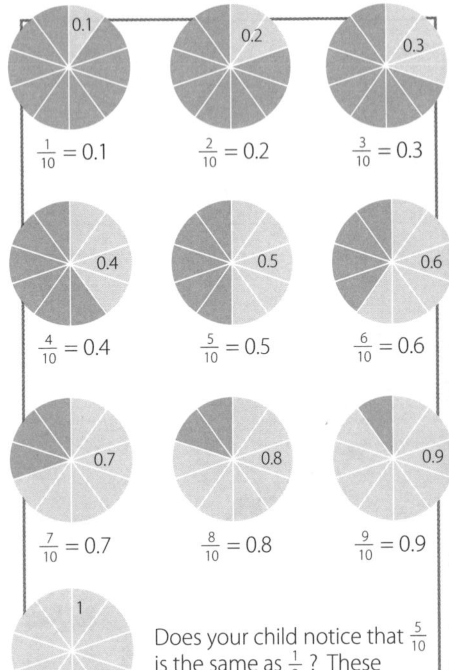

$\frac{10}{10} = 1$

Does your child notice that $\frac{5}{10}$ is the same as $\frac{1}{2}$? These fractions are equivalent.

Adding and subtracting

Don't forget to keep practising addition and subtraction facts. This is something that you could do with your child as you walk to school or travel in the car. Ask questions such as '13 add 8' or '32 subtract 7'. If your child finds these easy, that's very good news and you can encourage them to answer as quickly as possible. If your child finds this type of question difficult, keep practising and helping where necessary – practice really does make a difference.

When you feel that your child is confident with the addition and subtraction facts up to 20, move on to questions involving decimals, such as 'three add four-point-six'. This type of question will reveal whether your child understands 'place value' – that is, what each digit represents in a number.

You could move on to questions such as: 2.4 + 1.3

Then questions where the tenths will add up to enough to create an extra unit: 3.8 + 2.9

Try lots of questions such as these:

2 + 3.1 | 6 + 4.9
5.4 + 7 | 2.7 + 9

4.2 + 2.1 | 6.3 + 3.4
8.6 + 4.1 | 12.5 + 7.3

4.5 + 3.5 | 7.5 + 2.5
8.5 + 4.5 | 14.5 + 5.5

6.8 + 5.7 | 9.4 + 7.9
8.8 + 4.5 | 15.9 + 8.4

Subtracting decimals from 10 provides excellent practice for understanding decimals. Try questions such as:

10 – 4.5 | 10 – 7.3 | 10 – 3.9
10 – 9.6 | 10 – 2.5 | 10 – 6.4
10 – 1.7 | 10 – 0.8 | 10 – 5.2
10 – 8.1

Doubling and halving both help to improve mental arithmetic skills. Try asking these question:

Double 4.2 | Double 6.3
Double 2.1 | Double 5.4
Double 3.6 | Double 2.5
Double 7.6 | Double 8.9
Half of 7 | Half of 9
Half of 11 | Half of 19
Half of 8.4 | Half of 6.8
Half of 10.6 | Half of 14.2
Half of 9.6 | Half of 7.4
Half of 3.8 | Half of 5.2

Be careful, at this stage, not to ask questions such as 'half of 7.9', which will result in answers with two decimal places.

Written methods for addition

In Year 5 your child will be expected to 'use efficient written methods for addition and subtraction'.

As in Year 4, there may be several methods in use for adding together two numbers. Here are some of the methods your child may have been shown for adding:

Method 1: the empty number line

This is also shown in Year 4 on page 53:

459 + 276 = 735

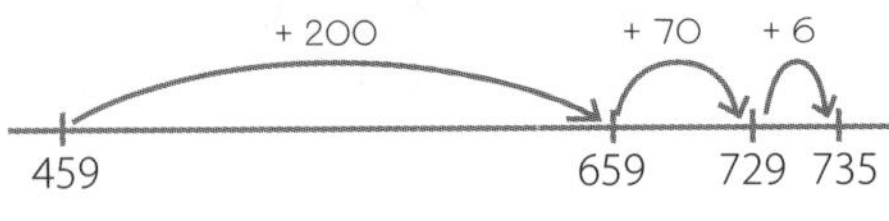

or

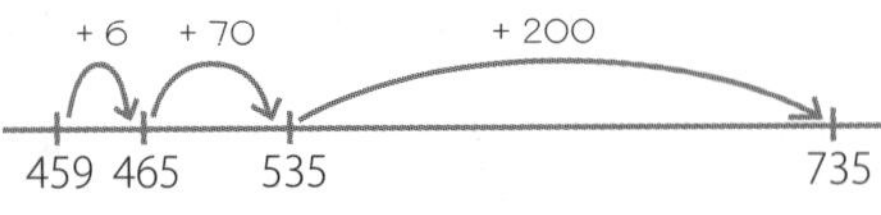

Method 2: partitioning

This is also shown in Year 4 on page 53:

459 + 276 =

400 + 200 + 50 + 70 + 9 + 6 =

600 + 120 + 15 =

720 + 15 =

735

Sometimes the partitioning method is shown like this:

```
  459        400 + 50 + 9
+ 276   =  + 200 + 70 + 6
           -------------
           600 + 120 + 15  = 735
```

Method 3: the expanded method

Some children may move on to an expanded method in columns.

```
  459            459
+ 276    or    + 276
-----          -----
  600             15
  120            120
   15            600
-----          -----
  735            735
```

Method 4: the column method

Some children will move on to the 'traditional' column method.

```
  459
+ 276
-----
  735
  11
```

All of these methods can be used with decimals and Year 5 pupils will be expected to add together decimals with up to two places.

Ask your child to show you how they complete some questions, using empty number lines, partitioning or any other method. It's a good idea to find out which of these methods the school uses, then encourage your child to use that method at home.

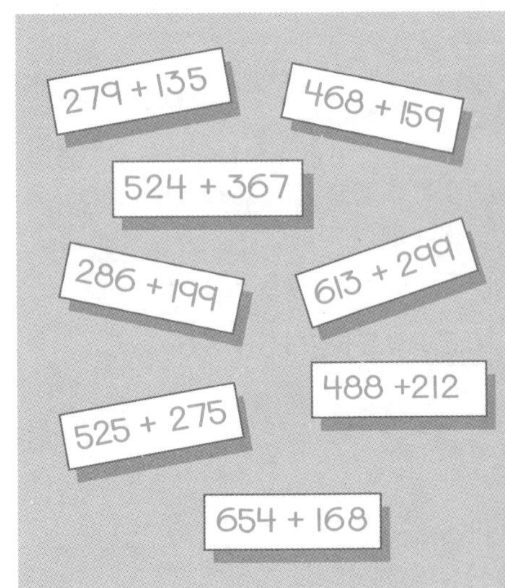

Written methods for subtraction

There are a number of methods that your child's school may use for teaching subraction.

Method 1: the empty number line – counting back

As in Year 4, the school may encourage the use of an empty number line for subtracting by counting back from the larger number to the smaller number:

629 – 342 = 287

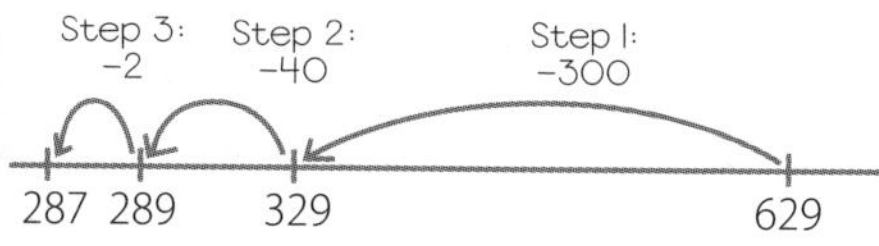

or

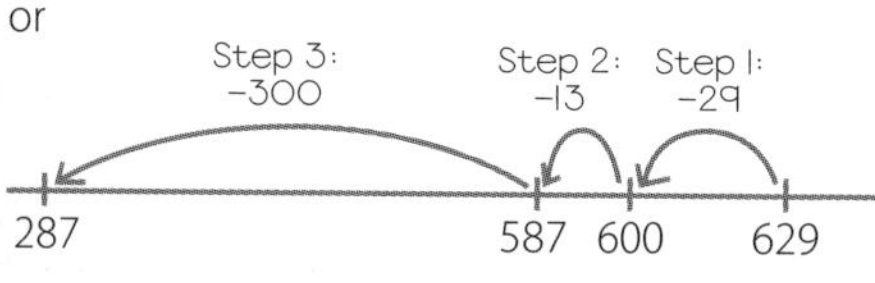

or

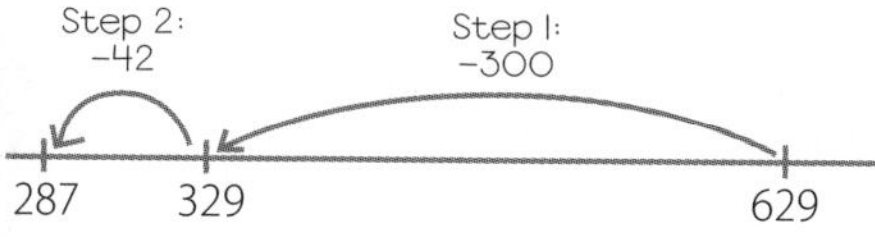

Method 2: the empty number line – counting up

The empty number line may also be used for counting up from the smaller number to the larger number:

629 – 342 = 287

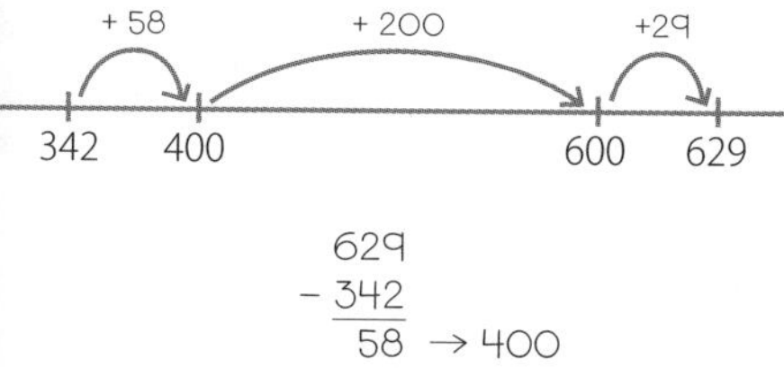


```
  629
- 342
   58 → 400
  200 → 600
   29 → 629
  287
```

or

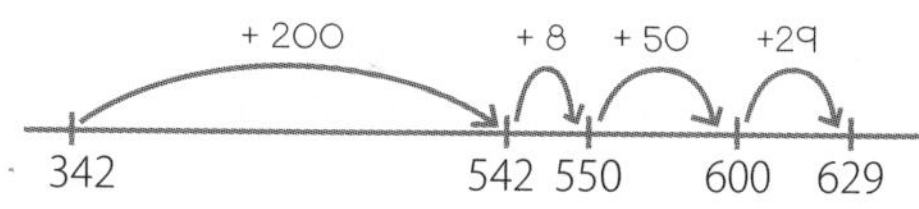


```
  629
- 342
  200 → 542
    8 → 550
   50 → 600
   29 → 629
  287
```

Notice the use of columns to record this process.

The number line method can also be used with decimals. For example, look how your child may be asked to subtract 26.7 from 34.5:

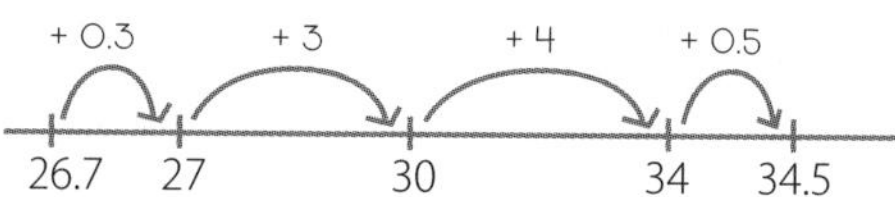

Again, the process may be shown in a column format.

```
   34.5
 – 26.7
    0.3 → 27
    3.0 → 30
    4.0 → 34
    0.5   34.5
    7.8
```

Here is an alternative approach using an empty number line, with the recording shown in a column format:

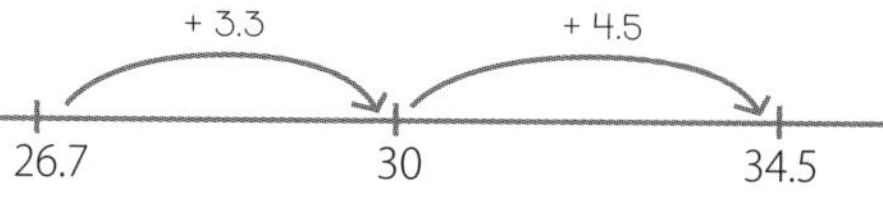


```
 34.5
 26.7
  3.3 → 30
  4.5 → 34.5
  7.8
```

Method 3: partitioning

Your child may be encouraged to use partitioning. We can take a look at the partitioning process with three different examples:

629 – 417, 629 – 342 and 625 - 287

Example 1: 629 – 417

$$\begin{array}{r} 629 \\ -\underline{417} \end{array} \rightarrow \begin{array}{r} 600 + 20 + 9 \\ -\ \underline{400 + 10 + 7} \\ 200 + 10 + 2 \end{array} = 212$$

In this example your child should start with subtracting the units (some schools call these 'ones'), then subtract the tens, then the hundreds. Most schools will recommend that the children say '20 take away 10' rather than '2 take away 1', and '600 take away 400' rather than '6 take away 4'. The school may choose to move on from this method to the more traditional layout:

$$\begin{array}{r} 629 \\ -\underline{417} \\ 212 \end{array}$$

Example 2: 629 – 342

$$\begin{array}{r} 629 \\ -\underline{342} \end{array} \rightarrow \begin{array}{r} 600 + 20 + 9 \\ -\ \underline{300 + 40 + 2} \end{array} \rightarrow$$

$$\begin{array}{r} 500 + 120 + 9 \\ -\ \underline{300 + 40 + 2} \\ 200 + 80 + 7 \end{array} = 287$$

Here your child can see that the 600 + 20 has been partitioned to make 500 + 120 so that the subtraction of the four tens will be '120 take away 40'. Again, the school may choose to move on from this method to the more traditional layout:

$$\begin{array}{r} {}^{5}\not{6}\,{}^{1}29 \\ -\underline{342} \\ 287 \end{array}$$

Example 3: 625 – 287

Look at this example where there are not enough units in 625 to subtract the 7 units in 287 and there are not enough tens in 625 to subtract the 80 in 287.

$$\begin{array}{r} 625 \\ -\underline{287} \end{array} \rightarrow \begin{array}{r} 600 + 20 + 5 \\ -\ \underline{200 + 80 + 7} \end{array} \rightarrow$$

$$\begin{array}{r} 500 + 110 + 15 \\ -\ \underline{200 + 80 + 7} \\ 300 + 30 + 8 \end{array} = 338$$

The 20 + 5 is partitioned into 10 + 15, then the 600 + 10 is partitioned into 500 + 110. This method leads to the more traditional layout:

$$\begin{array}{r} {}^{5}\not{6}\,{}^{11}\not{2}\,{}^{1}5 \\ -\ \underline{287} \\ 338 \end{array}$$

Ask your child to show you how they complete some questions, using empty number lines, partitioning or any other method. It's a good idea to find out which of these methods the school uses, then encourage your child to use that method at home.

465 – 132

989 – 387

756 – 324

638 – 211

536 – 282

681 – 266

714 – 365

900 – 328

Multiplying and dividing

As with adding and subtracting, it is a good idea to keep practising the multiplication tables.

Your child may have learnt all the multiplication tables in Year 4 but may have forgotten some of them. Try working on one table each week, starting with the ones your child may know already, the twos, threes, fours, fives and tens, then moving on to the sixes, sevens, eights and nines. Ask your child's teacher which table the children are working on so that you can practise that one at home.

The best way to learn each table is to practise for a short time every day – just one minute is enough. For example, if practising the 9 times-table, encourage your child to say:

One nine is nine

Two nines are eighteen

Three nines are twenty-seven

Four nines are thirty-six

Five nines are forty-five

Six nines are fifty-four

Seven nines are sixty-three

Eight nines are seventy-two

Nine nines are eighty-one

Ten nines are ninety

Discourage your child from only learning '9, 18, 27, 36, 45, 54, 63, 72, 81, 90'. It is quite useful to learn this number sequence but not nearly as useful as knowing, without hesitation, the answers to questions such as: 'six nines', 'three nines', 'eight nines' and so on.

Now ask your child lots of division questions, which make use of the tables. For example, you could ask:

- 'What's 36 divided by four?'
- 'Share 72 stickers between eight people'
- 'Divide 54 by six'

Written methods for multiplication

To help your child at home make sure that you are using the same method that is being taught at school. Ask your child's teacher to show you.

Here are some of the methods that the school may use: 64 x 7

Method 1: Informal recording

```
      64
  60  +  4
  ↓      ↓   x 7
 420  +  28  = 448
```

Method 2: the grid method

x	7
60	420
4	28
	448

Method 3: expanded short multiplication

```
  64
 x 7
 420    60 x 7 = 420
  28     4 x 7 =  28
 448
```

Method 4: short multiplication

```
  64
 x 7
 448
  2
```

Some schools will show the children all the methods, starting with method 1 and working through each of them. Method 4 is the method that most of us were taught at school but many schools choose not to use this, encouraging the children to be really successful with method 2 or method 3. The school will have a Calculation Policy and your child's class teacher should be able to tell you what this says in relation to multiplication.

Now look at how multiplication of two-digit numbers may be approached.

73 x 49

Your child will probably be asked to estimate the answer first. They will be encouraged to round both numbers to the nearest 10, then to multiply these approximations, ie 70 x 50. If your child knows their tables well they will probably work out that 70 x 50 = 3500.

Method 1: the grid method

Now they may use the grid method:

x	40	9	
70	2800	630	3430
3	120	27	147
			3577

Method 2: the column method

Or they may use a column method based on the grid method:

```
    73
  x 49
  2800     70 x 40 = 2800
   120      3 x 40 =  120
   630     70 x  9 =  630
    27      3 x  9 =   27
  3577
```

Method 3: the traditional column method

Or they may begin to use a column method that looks more like the one we used at school, but note that the children may multiply by the tens first rather than by the units first.

```
    73
  x 49
  2920     73 x 40
   657     73 x  9
  3577
```

Ask your child to show you how they complete some questions, using grids, an expanded method in columns or the 'traditional' column method. It's a good idea to find out which of these methods their school uses, then encourage your child to use that method at home.

82 x 27

49 x 34

26 x 26

98 x 46

72 x 38

65 x 19

25 x 25

19 x 19

Written methods for division

Here are some of the methods that the school may use:

Method 1: mental division using partitioning

96
↓
80 + 16
↓ ↓ ÷4
20 + 4 = 24

Method 2: partitioning with remainder

The partitioning method can also be used with questions that result in remainders.

77
↓
50 + 27
↓ ↓ ÷ 5
10 + 5r2 = 15r2

The partitioning method may be written out like this:

96 ÷ 4 = (80 + 16) ÷ 4
= (80 ÷ 4) + (16 ÷ 4)
= 20 + 4
= 24

Method 3: short division

This can lead to a method of short division that looks rather unfamiliar to most adults:

$$4\overline{)80+16} \quad \text{quotient } 20 + 4 = 24$$

This can be written in an even shorter way:

$$4\overline{)9^{1}6} \quad \text{quotient } 24$$

Method 4: chunking

But, what if your child needs to divide a three-digit number by a single-digit number? Your child may be encouraged to use 'partitioning', as shown on the previous page, or they may be asked to complete the division by 'chunking'. Although this appears strange it is very logical. Here is an example.

7⟌245
− 70   7 x 10
175
− 70   7 x 10
105
− 70   7 x 10
35
− 35   7 x 5
0   35

So 245 ÷ 7 = 35

If the children are confident with numbers, they may be asked to 'chunk' in a slightly different way:

7⟌245
− 210   7 x 30
35
− 35   7 x 5
0

So 245 ÷ 7 = 35

And if your child is really confident, especially with the partitioning process, they may be introduced to the short division method for dealing with three-digit numbers.

$$7\overline{)245} \quad = \quad 7\overline{)210 + 35} \quad \text{with } 30 + 5 = 35 \text{ above}$$

… which can be shortened to:

$$7\overline{)245} \quad = \quad \begin{array}{r} 35 \\ 7\overline{)24^{3}5} \end{array}$$

Note that this method can be used with questions that produce a remainder.

Ask your child to show you how they complete some questions, using partitioning, 'chunking' or any other method. It's a good idea to find out which of these methods their school uses, then encourage your child to use that method at home.

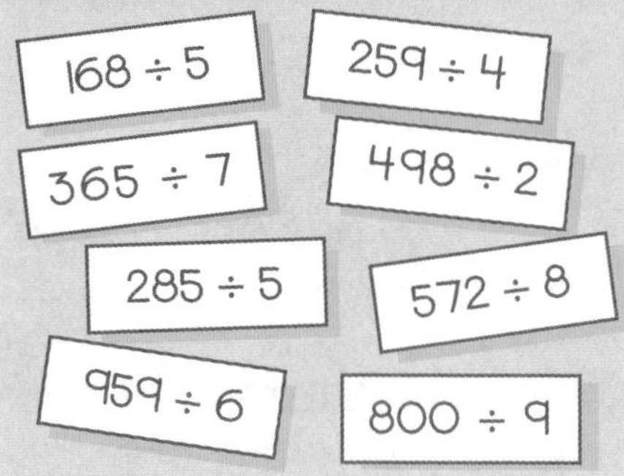

Looking at shapes

In Year 5 your child will learn more about the 2-D (two-dimensional) shapes that they have met before, and will be introduced to the idea of the scalene triangle.

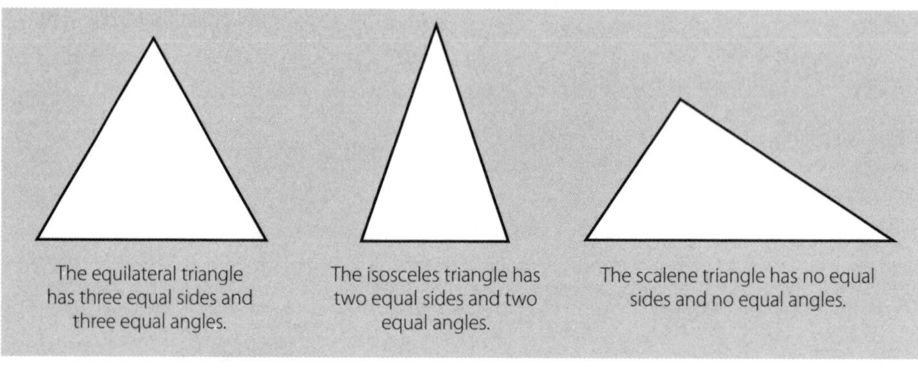

The equilateral triangle has three equal sides and three equal angles.

The isosceles triangle has two equal sides and two equal angles.

The scalene triangle has no equal sides and no equal angles.

They will continue to learn about 3-D (three-dimensional) shapes, including the octahedron.

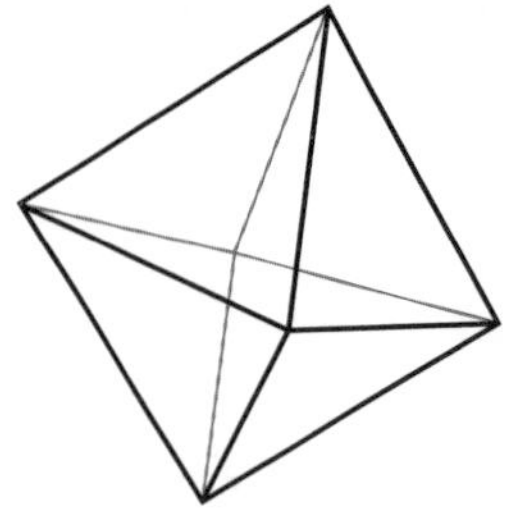

The octahedron has eight faces.

It's worth looking at packaging on supermarket shelves. Most items are packed in cuboid shaped boxes: cereal packets, washing powder and so on. Can your child find some unusual packaging materials? Encourage them to describe the shapes of the faces of the packing even if it's difficult to name the 3-D shape itself.

All about angles

Your child will need to be able to compare angles to a right angle and state whether they are acute or obtuse.

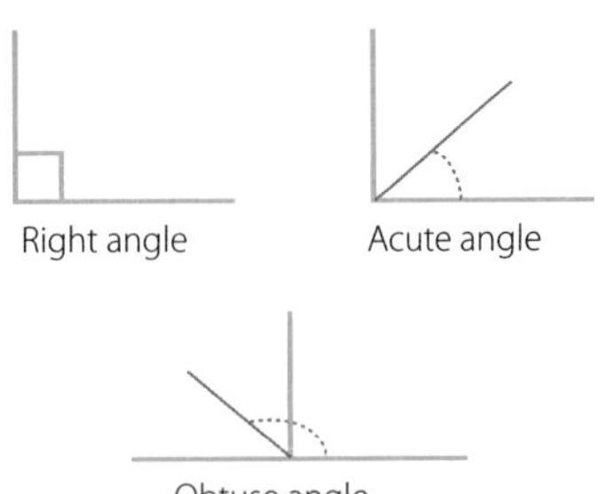

Right angle   Acute angle

Obtuse angle

They will be asked to calculate angles on a straight line. So, if an angle of 45° is shown, the children will have to calculate that the missing angle on the line is 135°.

45°   135°

Help your child with this at home by giving them some mental arithmetic questions based on subtracting from 180. Try questions such as:

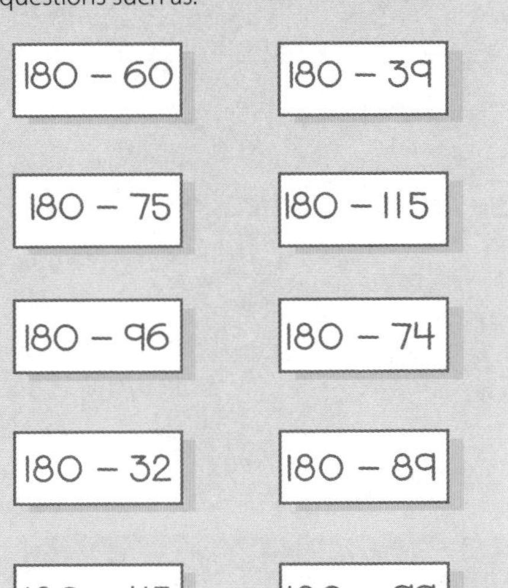

In Year 5 your child will use coordinates in the first quadrant (see page 62 for more information on this).

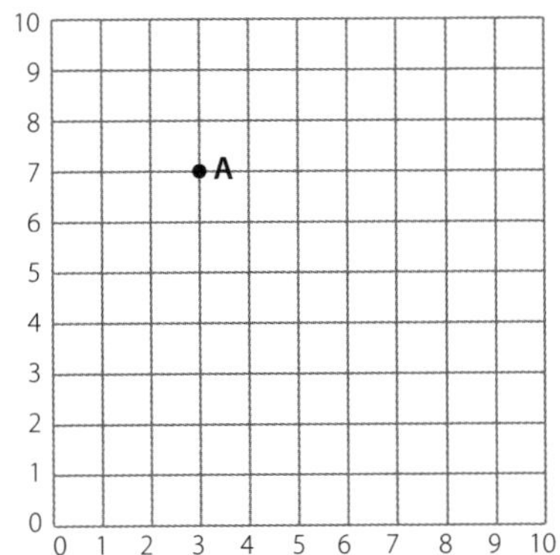

They will know that the position of the letter A on this grid can be given by the coordinates (3, 7) and will be aware how important it is to give the coordinate for the x-axis before the coordinate for the y-axis.

Many people like to remember which coordinate to find first by saying 'along the corridor and up the stairs' or 'find the eggs (x) before the yoghurt (y)'.

They may use the grid as part of their work for symmetry. For example, they may be asked to draw a reflection of a shape in a mirror line.

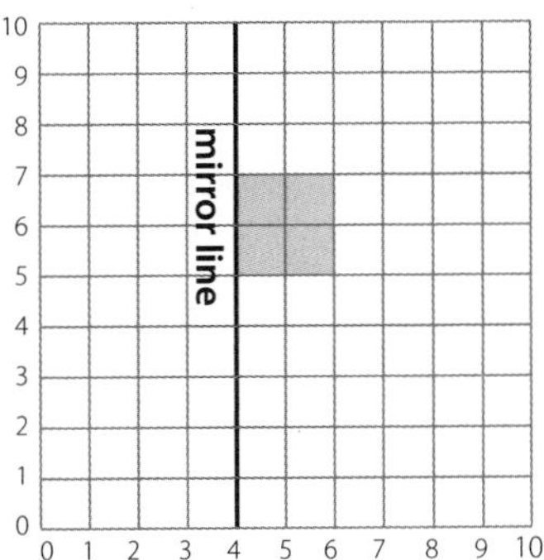

Draw half a house and ask your child to complete the picture to make the house completely symmetrical.

Measuring

Encourage your child to measure accurately using a ruler. Ask them:

'What is the length of each side of this hexagon?'

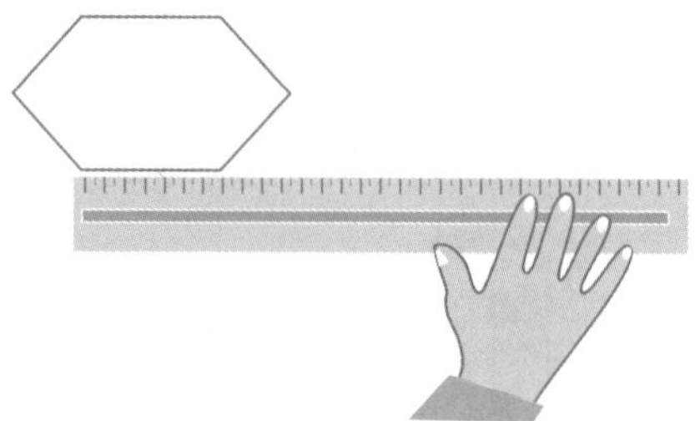

Encourage them to give the measurement in centimetres or centimetres and millimetres. Now ask them to work out the perimeter of the hexagon.

Ask your child to help weigh ingredients using kitchen scales.

Remind them to give the weight in grams or kilograms. Encourage your child to interpret the recipe that you are using. For example, if the recipe suggests using 100 grams to make six small muffins, how many grams would be needed to make three of these muffins or fifteen of these muffins?

Talking about time

Talk about the days of the week and the months of the year:

- 'Tell me the days of the week in order'
- 'Tell me the months of the year in order'
- 'How many days are there in each month?'
- 'How many days are there in a year?'
- 'How many days are there in a leap year?'

Help your child to tell the time accurately on a digital clock and to the nearest minute on an analogue (not digital) clock. You could compare the times on the two clocks. When using an analogue clock, encourage your child to say 'am' for morning times and 'pm' for any times after 12 noon. Now ask your child to say the same times using 24 hour clock notation.

Useful words

Take every opportunity to use other words associated with 'time', such as:

- morning
- afternoon
- evening
- night
- day
- week
- month
- year
- weekend
- birthday
- o'clock
- clock
- midnight
- half past
- hands
- seconds
- minutes
- hours
- century
- calendar
- date
- noon
- arrive
- depart
- 24-hour clock
- 12-hour clock

... and if your Year 5 child finds everything easy, have a look at what children are taught in Year 6.

Maths in Year 6

If your child is in Year 6 they will be expected to achieve targets for each aspect of mathematics. These are shown below, along with some quick and easy ways of helping your child with maths at home.

Using and applying mathematics

- ★ Solve problems that may have several steps.
- ★ Solve problems involving fractions, decimals or percentages.
- ★ Find the necessary information to solve a problem or puzzle and tabulate it systematically.
- ★ Check the accuracy of answers to questions.
- ★ Suggest lines of enquiry then plan and develop them.
- ★ Understand sequences, patterns and relationships involving numbers and shapes.

handy tip

Your child may be asked to identify the sequence of numbers called triangular numbers. Drawing the dots helps to show the sequence of numbers: 1, 3, 6, 10,and so on.

- ★ Begin to use algebra to create simple expressions and formulae.

The very word 'algebra' sends shivers down some people's spines! In fact, your child will have been working with algebra from a very early stage. A question such as $3 + \square = 7$ includes an empty box for the child to find the missing number: 4. When using 'algebra' your child may be faced with a question such as $3 + x = 7$, and will have to find the answer $x = 4$.

Counting and understanding numbers

- ★ Know that a whole number is called an integer.
- ★ Find the difference between a positive integer and a negative integer, or between two negative integers, in context – for example, temperature.
- ★ Express tenths, hundredths or thousandths as decimals.
- ★ Write decimal numbers in order. Show them in the correct places on a number line.
- ★ Understand mixed numbers. For example, know that $1\frac{3}{4}$ is the same as 7 quarters.

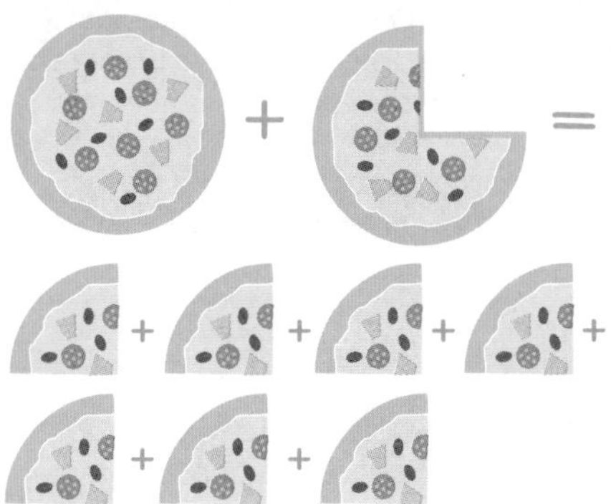

- ★ Simplify fractions.
- ★ Show one quantity as a percentage of another.
- ★ Find equivalent fractions, decimals and percentages.

Knowing and using number facts

- ★ Know the 2, 3, 4, 5, 6, 7, 8, 9 and 10 times-tables (see opposite).
- ★ Use the multiplication and division facts from the times-tables to find multiplication and division facts involving decimals.

Ask your child to find answers to questions such as 0.4 times 6. They will know that 4 x 6 = 24, so 0.4 x 6 = 2.4.

- ★ Find the square numbers: 1 x 1, 2 x 2, 3 x 3, 4 x 4, 5 x 5, 6 x 6, 7 x 7, 8 x 8, 9 x 9, 10 x 10, 11 x 11 and 12 x 12. Find the squares of multiples of 10, for example, 40 x 40.
- ★ Understand prime numbers and find prime numbers less than 100.

A prime number is a number that only has itself and 1 as factors – in other words it's not in any times-table except its own. So, for example, the number 7 is a prime number because it only appears as an answer in the 7 times-table and not in any other table. The number 9 is not prime because it's in the 3 times-table as well as the 9 times-table. The number 13 is prime, so are 17 and 19.

7 9 13 17

1 x 2 = 2
2 x 2 = 4
3 x 2 = 6
4 x 2 = 8
5 x 2 = 10
6 x 2 = 12
7 x 2 = 14
8 x 2 = 16
9 x 2 = 18
10 x 2 = 20

1 x 3 = 3
2 x 3 = 6
3 x 3 = 9
4 x 3 = 12
5 x 3 = 15
6 x 3 = 18
7 x 3 = 21
8 x 3 = 24
9 x 3 = 27
10 x 3 = 30

1 x 4 = 4
2 x 4 = 8
3 x 4 = 12
4 x 4 = 16
5 x 4 = 20
6 x 4 = 24
7 x 4 = 28
8 x 4 = 32
9 x 4 = 36
10 x 4 = 40

1 x 5 = 5
2 x 5 = 10
3 x 5 = 15
4 x 5 = 20
5 x 5 = 25
6 x 5 = 30
7 x 5 = 35
8 x 5 = 40
9 x 5 = 45
10 x 5 = 50

1 x 6 = 6
2 x 6 = 12
3 x 6 = 18
4 x 6 = 24
5 x 6 = 30
6 x 6 = 36
7 x 6 = 42
8 x 6 = 48
9 x 6 = 54
10 x 6 = 60

1 x 7 = 7
2 x 7 = 14
3 x 7 = 21
4 x 7 = 28
5 x 7 = 35
6 x 7 = 42
7 x 7 = 49
8 x 7 = 56
9 x 7 = 63
10 x 7 = 70

1 x 8 = 8
2 x 8 = 16
3 x 8 = 24
4 x 8 = 32
5 x 8 = 40
6 x 8 = 48
7 x 8 = 56
8 x 8 = 64
9 x 8 = 72
10 x 8 = 80

1 x 9 = 9
2 x 9 = 18
3 x 9 = 27
4 x 9 = 36
5 x 9 = 45
6 x 9 = 54
7 x 9 = 63
8 x 9 = 72
9 x 9 = 81
10 x 9 = 90

1 x 10 = 10
2 x 10 = 20
3 x 10 = 30
4 x 10 = 40
5 x 10 = 50
6 x 10 = 60
7 x 10 = 70
8 x 10 = 80
9 x 10 = 90
10 x 10 = 100

Calculating

★ Use mental arithmetic for a range of calculations with integers and decimals.

★ Use efficient written methods for addition and subtraction of both integers and decimals.

★ Use efficient written methods for multiplying integers and decimals by a one-digit integer and for multiplying two-digit integers and three-digit integers by a two-digit integer.

★ Use efficient written methods for dividing integers and decimals by a one-digit integer.

★ Find fractions of numbers or quantities.

★ Find percentages of numbers and quantities.

Ask your child to find 10% of a certain amount, for example, £60. They should know straight away that 10% is the same as one tenth and so 10% of £60 = £6. Now ask for 5% of £60. Well, that must be half of 10% so it's £3. Now ask for 15%. That must be 10% plus 5%, that's £6 plus £3 so 15% of £60 = £9. Finding 20% can be done by doubling the 10% and so on.

★ Use a calculator efficiently.

Understanding shape

★ Understand and use parallel and perpendicular edges or faces.

parallel lines never meet

perpendicular lines meet at right angles

★ Draw shapes accurately.

★ Draw reflections and rotations of shapes on grids.

★ Use coordinates in the first quadrant.

For more information on the term 'quadrant' see page 62.

★ Estimate the sizes of angles.

★ Use a protractor.

Many children make mistakes using protractors simply because they haven't started measuring from the zero marker. There are two zero markers on the protractor and they have to decide which one to line up with the angle they're measuring – once they've decided they have to follow the measurements around the protractor from the zero they've chosen.

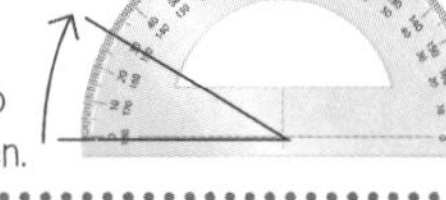

★ Calculate angles in a triangle.

★ Calculate angles around a point.

Measuring

★ Use appropriate metric units to estimate and measure.

Please note that your child will use metric units in school so it's best to practise with these at home. Life is much simpler with metres, centimetres and so on rather than yards, feet and inches!

★ Convert between units to two decimal places. For example, convert 1.64 metres to 164 centimetres or to 1640 millimetres.

★ Interpret scales on measuring instruments.

★ Calculate the perimeters and areas of shapes made from rectangles.

★ Estimate the areas of irregular shapes by counting squares on a grid.

Handling data

★ Discuss events using vocabulary related to chance or likelihood.

★ Collect data and organize it to answer a set of related questions.

★ Draw frequency tables, pictograms, bar graphs and line graphs.

★ Interpret pie charts.

Favourite pets

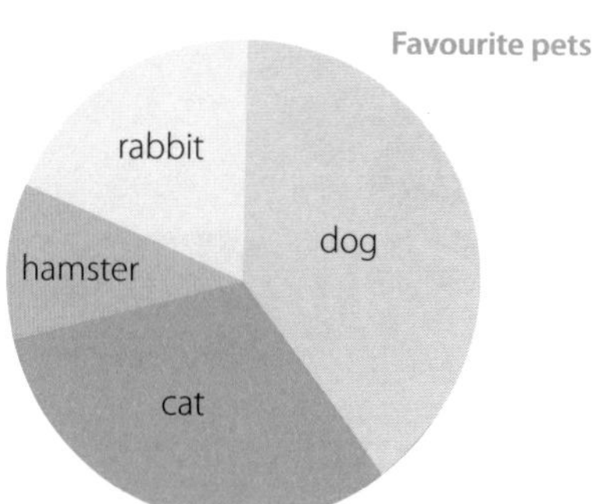

★ Find the mode, range, median and mean of a set of data and explain what they show.

Look at the following numbers of goals scored by the school netball team in seven matches:
1 6 2 4 2 4 2
The mode is 2 because it appears most often (sometimes data won't have a mode). The range is 5, because it is the largest piece of data minus the smallest: 6 – 1 = 5. To find the median you put the data in order: 1 2 2 2 4 4 6 then choose the middle piece: 2. To find the mean you add all the data together then divide by the number of pieces of data: 1 + 6 + 2 + 4 + 2 + 4 + 2 = 21
21 ÷ 7 = 3 so the mean is 3.

How else can I help at home?

It's important to make maths as much fun as possible and to use lots of repetition. Talk to your child's class teacher to ensure that you know what your child should be practising.

Using and applying mathematics

At the garage

To encourage your child in 'using and applying mathematics' take every opportunity to talk about maths in everyday life. This might be, for example, when filling the car with petrol. Try the following:

- Ask your child to watch the pump, so that they can see the cost rising as the number of litres rises.
- Can they interpret the pump correctly, noticing the use of a decimal point in both the cost part of the pump and in the quantity part?

It's a good idea to relate the use of negative numbers to some real-life examples. Temperature is ideal for this. Look together at an outdoor thermometer, noting the position of 0° Celsius, then talk about the temperatures below zero.

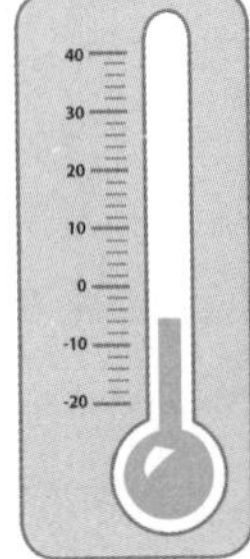

A great activity is to go on to the Internet and find temperatures in different parts of the world, then to compare these to the temperature at home.

Counting and understanding numbers

Practise counting backwards with your child from 20, but continue beyond 0 to the negative numbers. Note that many schools will refer to 'negative 1', 'negative 2', and so on, rather than 'minus 1', 'minus 2' and so on.

Your child's school may refer to the whole numbers as 'integers' – ask your child if they are familiar with this word.

−7 −6 −5 −4 −3 −2 −1 0 1 2 3 4 5 6 7 8 9 10 11 12

← negative numbers → ← positive numbers →

Fraction fun

Talk about relating familiar fractions to their decimal equivalents. Your child should know all those shown on page 64 in our section about Year 5.

They should know how to express various fractions as decimals. Look at these examples involving hundredths:

$\frac{1}{100} = \mathbf{0.01}$ $\frac{7}{100} = \mathbf{0.07}$

$\frac{12}{100} = \mathbf{0.12}$ $\frac{35}{100} = \mathbf{0.35}$

$\frac{25}{100} = \mathbf{0.25}$ $\frac{50}{100} = \mathbf{0.5}$

$\frac{75}{100} = \mathbf{0.75}$

Try writing each of these on separate pieces of card then ask your child to match the pairs. Once they can do these easily add more cards into the mix.

These examples involve thousandths:

$\frac{1}{1000} = \mathbf{0.001}$ $\frac{6}{1000} = \mathbf{0.006}$

$\frac{25}{1000} = \mathbf{0.025}$ $\frac{98}{1000} = \mathbf{0.098}$

$\frac{214}{1000} = \mathbf{0.214}$ $\frac{250}{1000} = \mathbf{0.25}$

$\frac{500}{1000} = \mathbf{0.5}$ $\frac{750}{1000} = \mathbf{0.75}$

Your child will use mixed numbers:

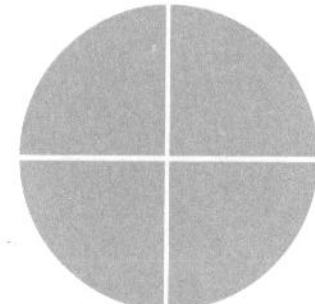

They will be expected to understand that the amount shaded above could be represented in three ways:

$\mathbf{1\frac{3}{4}}$ $\frac{7}{4}$ **1.75**

Fuel fractions

It's a good idea to give your child practice in finding fractions of quantities. For example, you could find out how much fuel your car holds when its tank is full. Ask your child to work out how much is in the tank when it's half full, quarter full or three quarters full. Extend this by asking your child to find the cost of half a tank of fuel by referring to the price of fuel at the filling station.

Adding and subtracting

Decimal dilemmas

If you feel that your child is confident with the addition and subtraction facts up to 20, move on to questions involving decimals, such as 'seven add two-point-four'. This type of question will reveal whether your child understands 'place value' – that is, what each digit represents in a number.

You could move on to questions such as:

5.8 + 2.1

Then questions where the tenths will add up to enough to create an extra unit:

3.8 + 2.9

Then questions involving three numbers.

Try lots of questions such as these:

4 + 2.7 + 1.3

9 + 2.5 + 1.4

8.2 + 3.6 + 1.7

16 + 9.5 + 3.8

18 + 7.8 + 2.9

17 + 4.4 + 4.1

27 + 6.3 + 5.2

36 + 5.1 + 4.5

47 + 8.2 + 6.6

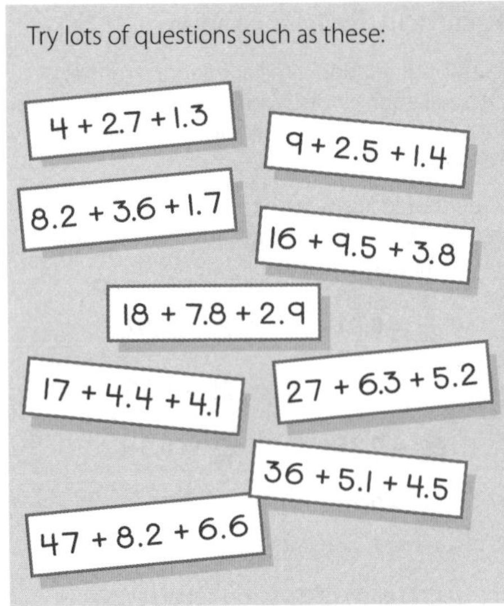

Activity ideas Change please!

Challenge your child to pretend they are working in a shop and you are an awkward customer who only has a £10 note to pay for anything! See if they can work out the correct change to give you. This provides excellent practice for understanding decimals. Try questions such as:

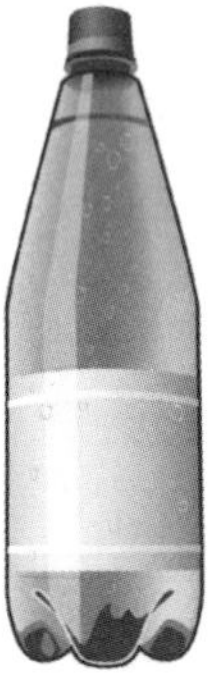

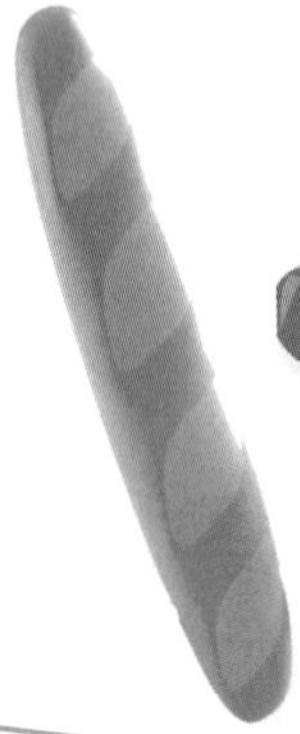

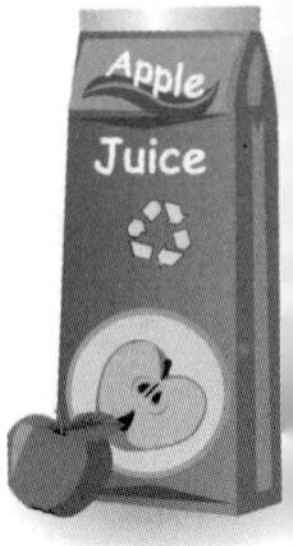

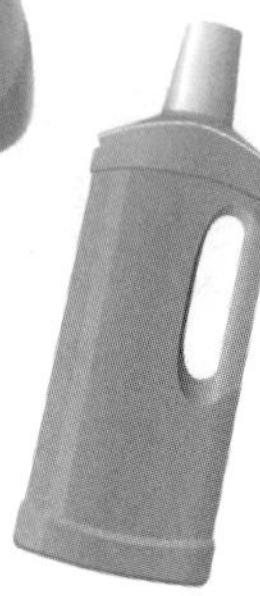

£10 – £4.58

£10 – £7.98

£10 – £2.14

£10 – £5.32

£10 – £9.66

£10 – £8.99

£10 – £6.83

£10 – £2.41

£10 – £1.67

£10 – £3.75

£10 – 35p

Written methods for addition

In Year 6 your child will be expected to 'use efficient written methods for addition and subtraction' of both integers and decimals. Most schools will use the 'traditional' column method with pupils of this age:

```
  496
+ 378
  874
  1 1
```

But I certainly know of some schools that continue to use some of the other methods as shown on page 53 or page 66 . It's worth checking with your child's teacher to find out which method is used. The school should have developed a calculation policy so that all the teachers know which methods to use with the children in their class.

The column method is very successful with decimal numbers provided the child enters the digits in the correct columns.

These are some examples of adding that I've seen used by children:

```
  14          14.0          14
+  3.6   ✓  +  3.6   ✓  +  3.6   ✗
  17.6        17.6          5.0
```

If your child is very successful with these questions, try finding change from £100:

£100 – £32.48

£100 – £25.50

£100 – £69.42

£100 – £78.64

£100 – £83.29

£100 – £1.47

£100 – £29.61

£100 – £12.13

£100 – £74.36

£100 – £93.45

Written methods for subtraction

As there are a range of methods that may be used for subtraction, find out from your child's class teacher which method they are using.

Method 1: the empty number line

Some schools will continue to use the number line method for working with decimals. For example, look how your child may be asked to subtract 38.4 from 52.6:

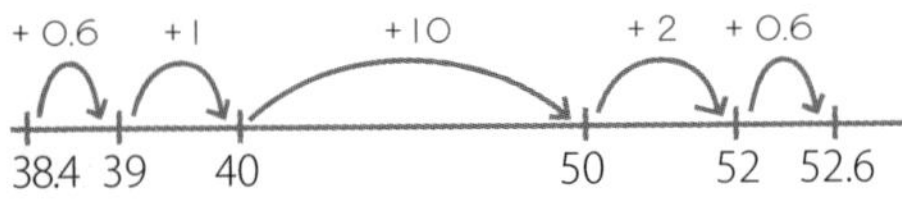

Again, the process may be shown in a column format:

```
  52.6
- 38.4
   0.6 → 39
   1.0 → 40
  10.0 → 50
   2.0 → 52
   0.6 → 52.6
  14.2
```

Here is an alternative approach using an empty number line, with the recording shown in a column format:

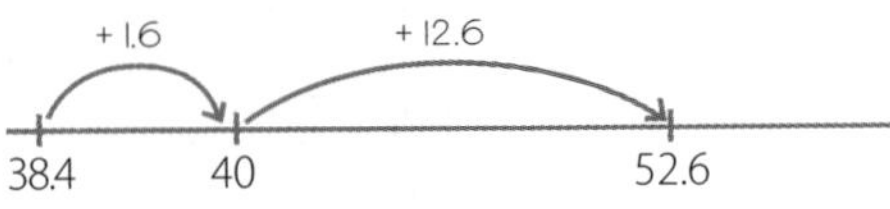


```
  52.6
- 38.4
   1.6 → 40
  12.6 → 52.6
  14.2
  1
```

Method 2: partitioning

Your child may be encouraged to use partitioning, leading on to a more compact column method:

634 – 278

```
  600 + 30 + 4          500 + 120 + 14
- 200 + 70 + 8   →    - 200 +  70 +  8
                        300 +  50 +  6

        5 12 1
        6  3 4
  →   - 2  7 8
        3  5 6
```

Look at this example, which involves dealing with a zero in the larger number:

704 – 387

```
  700 +  0 + 4          600 + 90 + 14
- 300 + 80 + 7   →    - 300 + 80 +  7
                        300 + 10 +  7

        6 9 1
        7 0 4
  →   - 3 8 7
        3 1 7
```

Method 3: the 'traditional' column method

Many schools will now be using the 'traditional' method in columns:

562 – 347

```
   5 1
  5 6 2
- 3 4 7
  2 1 5
```

Ask your child to show you the method used in their class. How would they answer the following questions?

843 – 297	624 – 182
912 – 148	406 – 132
740 – 256	900 – 357
518 – 324	809 – 165

Multiplying and dividing

As with adding and subtracting, it's a good idea to keep practising the times-tables.

Your child may have learnt all the times-tables in Year 4 and Year 5 but may have forgotten some of them. Try working on one table each week, starting with the ones they may know already, the twos, threes, fours, fives and tens, then moving on to the sixes, sevens, eights and nines. Ask your child's teacher which table the children are working on so that you can practise the same one at home.

The best way to learn each table is to practise for a short time every day – just one minute is enough. For example, if practising the 8 times-table, encourage your child to say:

One eight is eight

Two eights are sixteen

Three eights are twenty-four

Four eights are thirty-two

Five eights are forty

Six eights are forty-eight

Seven eights are fifty-six

Eight eights are sixty-four

Nine eights are seventy-two

Ten eights are eighty.

Discourage your child from only learning '8, 16, 24, 32, 40, 48, 56, 64, 72, 80. It is quite useful to learn this number sequence but not nearly as useful as knowing, without hesitation, the answers to questions such as: 'three eights', 'seven eights', 'nine eights' and so on.
Now ask your child lots of division questions, which make use of the tables. Try:

- 'What's 32 divided by 4?'
- 'Divide 56 by 8.'
- '72 divided by 8'.
- 'How many eights are there in 64?'

And some with remainders:

- 34 divided by 8.
- 41 divided by 8.
- Divide 77 by 8.

Written methods for multiplication

To help your child at home make sure that you are using the same method that is being taught in their class. Ask the teacher to show you.

Here are some of the methods that the school may use for 56 x 9:

Method 1: informal recording

```
    56
 50  +  6
 ↓      ↓  x 9
450  + 54  = 504
```

Method 2: the grid method

x	9
50	450
6	54
	504

Method 3: expanded short multiplication

```
  56
 x 9
 450     50 x 9 = 450
  54      6 x 9 =  54
 504
```

Method 4: short multiplication

```
  56
 x 9
 504
  5
```

Some schools will show the children all the methods, starting with method 1 and working through each of them. Method 4 is the method that most of us were taught at school but many schools choose not to use this, encouraging the children to be really successful with method 2 or method 3. The school will have a Calculation Policy and your child's teacher should be able to tell you what this says in relation to multiplication.

Now look at how the multiplication of two-digit numbers may be approached.

Example: 58 x 42

Your child will probably be asked to estimate the answer first. They will be encouraged to round both numbers to the nearest 10, then to multiply these approximations, that is, 60 x 40. If your child knows their tables well they will probably work out that 60 x 40 = 2400.

Method 1: the grid method

Now they may use the grid method.

x	40	2	
50	2000	100	2100
8	320	16	336
			2436

Method 2: the column method

Or they may use a column method based on the grid method:

```
   58
 x 42
 2000     50 x 40 = 2000
  320      8 x 40 =  320
  100     50 x  2 =  100
   16      8 x  2 =   16
 2436
```

Method 3: the traditional column method

Or they may begin to use a column method that looks more like the one we used at school, but note that the children may multiply by the tens first rather than by the units first.

Look at this example where a three-digit number is being multiplied by a two-digit number.

```
   396
×   28
  7920
  3168
   7 4
 11088
```

Ask your child to show you how they complete some questions. It's a good idea to find out which of these methods the school uses, then encourage your child to use that method at home.

249 × 32	456 × 38
629 × 57	586 × 99

Written methods for division

Here are some of the methods that the school may use:

Method 1: mental division using partitioning

```
    91
    ↓
70  +  21
↓      ↓   ÷ 7
10  +  3   = 13
```

This method can also be used with questions that result in remainders.

Method 2: partitioning with remainder

```
    87
    ↓
60  +  27
↓      ↓   ÷ 6
10  +  4r3 = 14r3
```

The partitioning method may be written out like this:

$$91 \div 7 = (70 + 21) \div 7$$
$$= (70 \div 7) + (21 \div 7)$$
$$= 10 + 3$$
$$= 13$$

Method 3: short division

This can lead to short division. Look at how 91 might be divided by 4.

```
  20 + 2 r3 = 22 r3
4|80 + 11
```

This can be written in an even shorter way:

```
  22 r3
4|9¹1
```

Now look at how dividing a three-digit number by a single-digit number may be approached.

Method 1: chunking

There is an example of 'chunking' in the Year 5 section on page 71. Here is another example.

```
8⌐362
  - 80     8 x 10
   282
  - 80     8 x 10
   202
  - 80     8 x 10
   122
    80     8 x 10
    42
  - 40     8 x 5
    r2        45
```

So $362 \div 8 = 45$ r2

If the children are confident with numbers, they may be asked to 'chunk' in a slightly different way:

```
8⌐362
 - 320    8 x 40
    42
  - 40    8 x  5
     2        45
```

So $362 \div 8 = 45$ r2

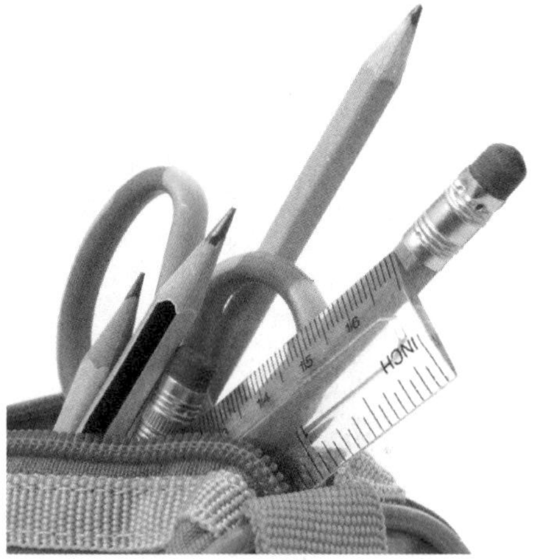

Method 2: short division

And if the children are really confident, especially with the partitioning process, they may be introduced to the short division method for dealing with three-digit numbers.

```
                 40 +    5r2 = 45 r2
8⌐362   =   8⌐320 + 45
```

... which can be shortened to:

```
   45 r2
8⌐36⁴2
```

Ask your child to show you how they complete some questions. It's a good idea to find out which of these methods the school uses, then encourage your child to use that method at home.

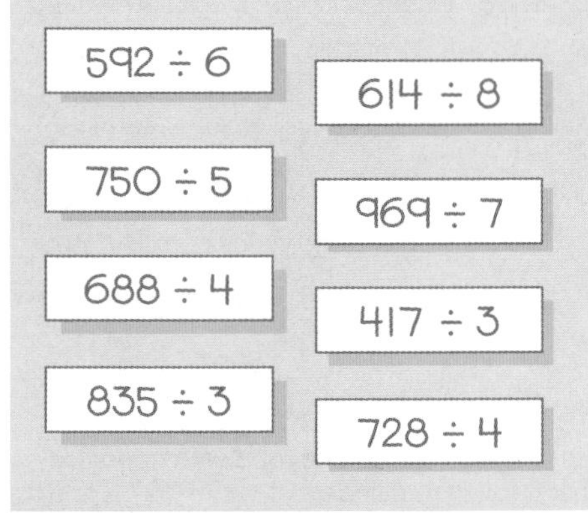

Long division

Your child may be introduced to long division in Year 6. This may be linked to the chunking method. Your child will again be encouraged to make estimates for answers.

Look at this example: **598 ÷ 14**

Your child will be encouraged to multiply 14 by multiples of 10:

$10 \times 14 = 140$

$20 \times 14 = 280$

$30 \times 14 = 420$

$40 \times 14 = 560$

$50 \times 14 = 700$

They can see that the number 598 is somewhere between 560 and 700, so the 560 is subtracted from the 598:

```
14|598
 - 560    14 x 40
    38
 -  28    14 x  2
    10
```

So $598 \div 14 = 42$ r10

This is actually quite similar to the 'traditional' long division method:

```
     42
14|598
 - 560
    38
 -  28
    10
```

$598 \div 14 = 42$ r10

Notice that your child will still be encouraged to think about 'chunks', so they are reminded that the 4 in the answer represents 40 lots of 14 – for this reason, 560 is subtracted from 598 at the point highlighted in green.

Looking at shapes

Children in Year 6 will learn more about the 2-D (two-dimensional) shapes that they have discussed before, and will be introduced to the rhombus, the kite, the parallelogram and the trapezium.

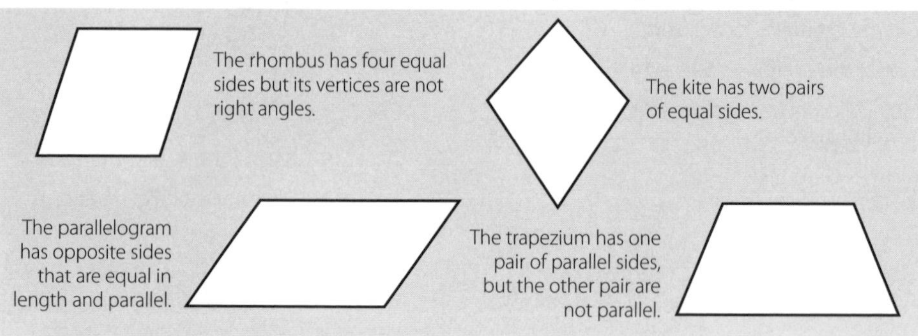

They will also be introduced to the dodecahedron, a 3-D (three-dimensional) shape with 12 faces.

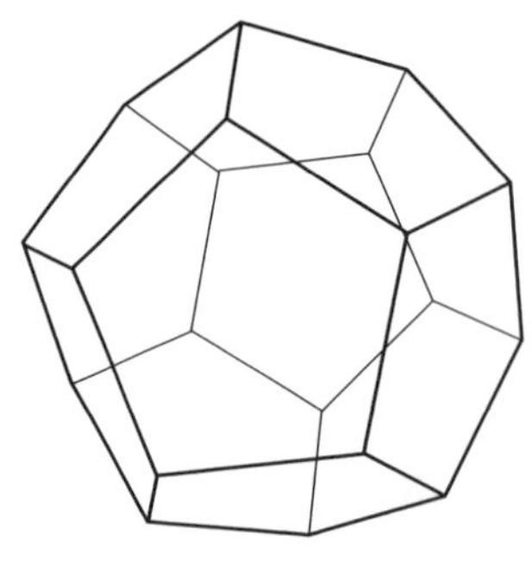

Shape hunt

Try looking for 3-D shapes when out and about. Does any of the architecture in your town include any unusual shapes? It's surprising what you may find:

- church spires are sometimes cones or pyramids
- water towers may be cylinders
- roofs are often triangular prisms.

Supermarket shelves also provide opportunities for finding 3-D shapes.

All about angles

Your child will be asked to measure angles using a protractor – a notoriously difficult operation! Help them to practise this at home.

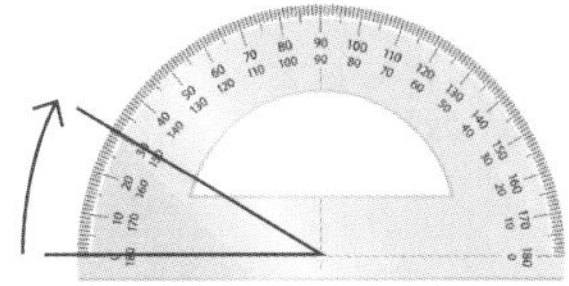

In fact, it's not so difficult if some simple rules are followed:

1. Line up the 'cross' on the protractor with the point of the angle.
2. Line up one of the zero lines on the protractor with one of the lines of the angle to be measured. (Look at the protractor: one of the zeroes is at the start of the inner ring of numbers and the other is at the start of the outer ring of numbers.)
3. Measure from the zero line that you have matched to the line of the angle, not from the other one! (This is where children make the most errors: they line up the protractor very carefully then measure from the wrong set of numbers.)

Angles in a triangle

In their class, your child will be asked to calculate the angles in a triangle. They will be shown triangles with two angles provided and they will have to work out the size of the third angle.

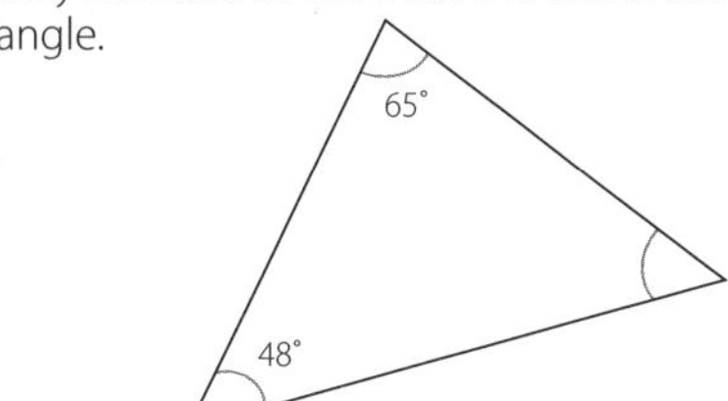

To complete this question your child would have to follow two steps:

1. Add the two angles shown together.
2. Subtract the answer from 180°

Subtracting from 180° is a very useful mental arithmetic skill – practise this using the questions on page 73 in the Year 5 section.

Sometimes your child may be asked to find the size of an angle in a special type of triangle. Look at these two examples:

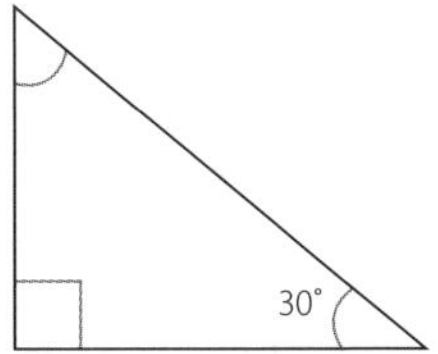

Here, your child should notice that they have been provided with the size of two angles: the 30° angle but also the right angle, which is of course 90°. So again, they need to add these together and subtract from 180°.

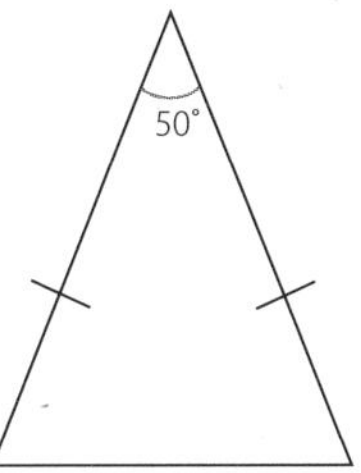

Here, the children should notice that this is an isosceles triangle so two of the angles will be equal.

In Year 6, your child will learn that the angles around a point add up to 360˚.

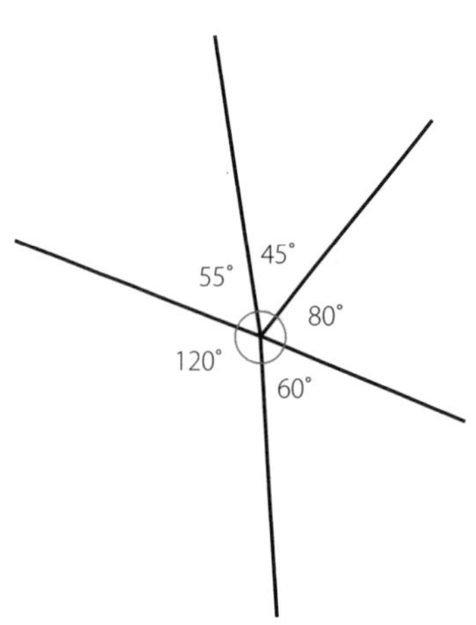

So they may be asked to find a missing angle:

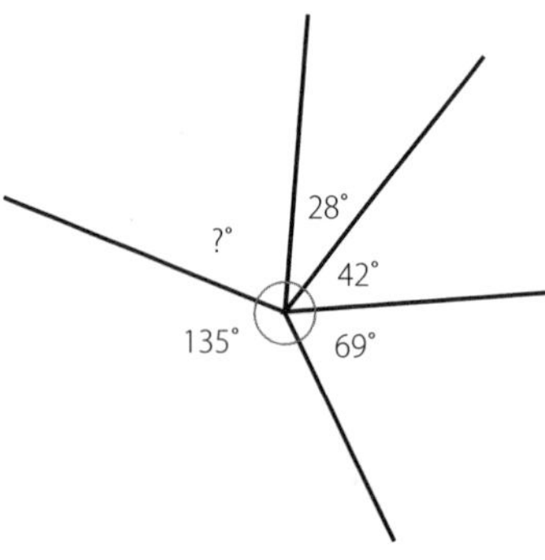

It is perfectly acceptable to use a calculator to add together the sizes of the angles provided, then to subtract from 360º.

Measuring

Encourage your child to measure accurately using a ruler, weighing scales and measuring jugs.

In Year 6 your child may be asked to find the perimeter of shapes built from rectangles:

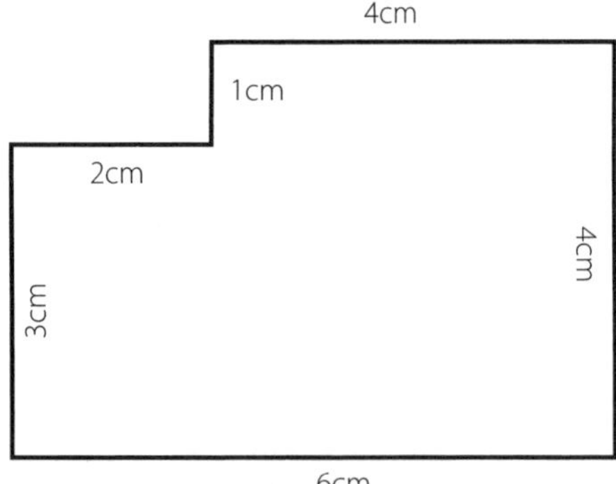

The total perimeter is 20cm.

And they may be asked to find the area of the same shape. This can be done by splitting the shape into two rectangles, finding the area of each, then adding these together.

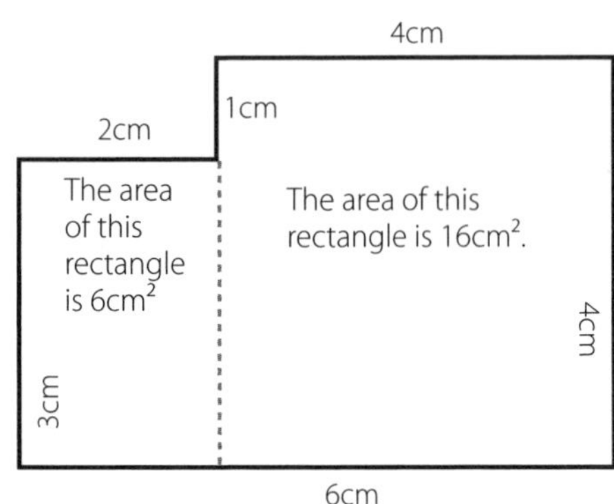

The total area is $22cm^2$.

Ask your child to find the perimeter and area of each of these shapes. Make sure that they write the perimeter in centimetres (cm) and the area in square centimetres (cm^2).

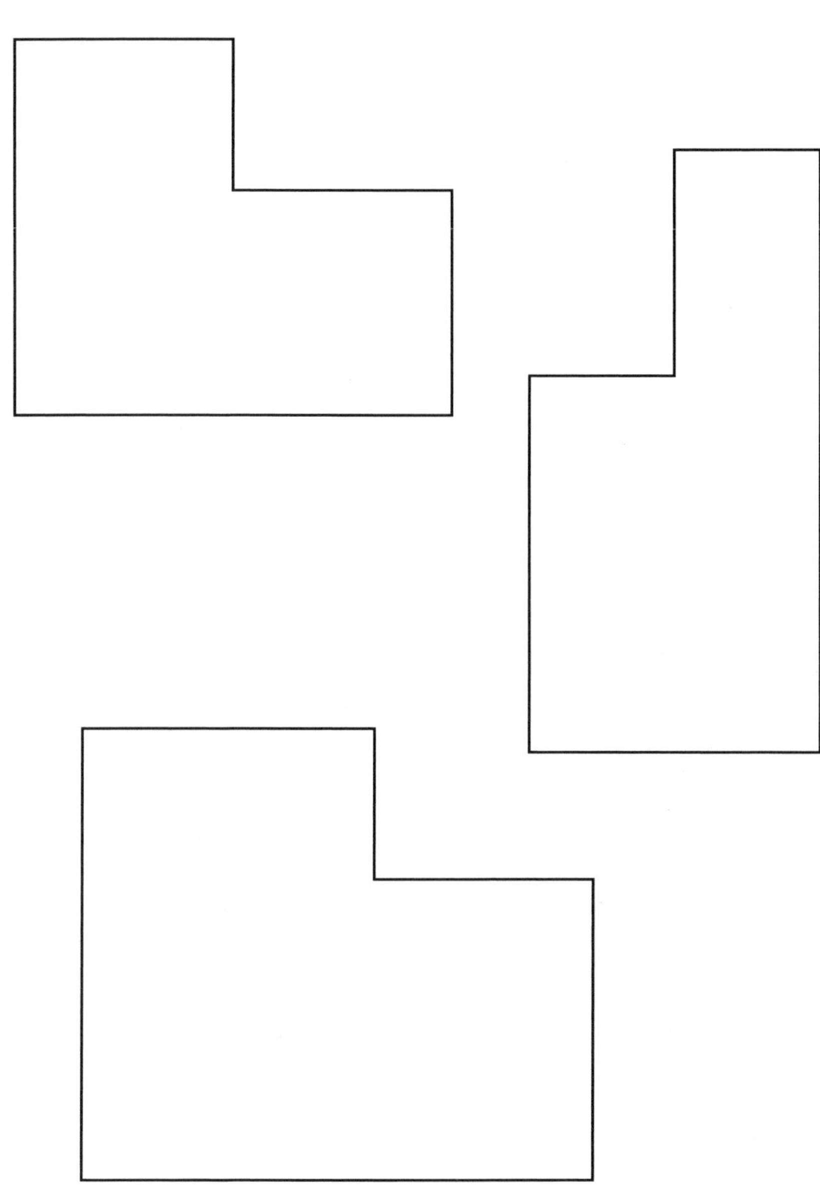

Author note

I do hope that this book has been of help to you in understanding the type of maths that your child is taught in primary school. I have not been able to include every aspect of maths in such a slim volume so you may decide to ask your child's teacher for further guidance.

In my view, children are likely to be much more successful in maths if they have a strong foundation of number skills and you may be interested in some of my other books to help your child with this.

Of course, these skills are of little value if your child doesn't know how to apply them. You can help by making sure you bring maths into your everyday activities such as shopping, cooking, travelling, DIY and craft work.

Andrew Brodie

ENJOY YOUR MATHS TOGETHER!